PRAISE FOR

7

"Sus
base
Gos
exp
asp
or (

"T
te
fii
le
n
k
(

DATE DUE			

r

1
k
ft

"For a leader who seeks to be a great leader, the truths found in Bob Goshen's new book will set you free."

Grant Teaff
Executive Director, AFCA
Author, *Grant Teaff with the Master Coaches*

"What the world needs now is visionary leadership that leads. *The Power of Layered Leadership* teaches how to do that effectively through all creative levels."

Mark Victor Hansen
Co-creater, #1 New York Times best
selling series *Chicken Soup for the Soul®*,
Co-author, *Cracking the Millionaire Code*,
The One Minute Millionaire, and *Cash in a Flash*,
Author, *Richest Kids in America*

THE POWER OF
LAYERED
LEADERSHIP

BOB GOSHEN

THE POWER OF
LAYERED
LEADERSHIP

HOW TO DISCOVER, DEVELOP,
& DUPLICATE LEADERS

TATE PUBLISHING & *Enterprises*

Published by Tate Publishing & Enterprises, LLC
127 E. Trade Center Terrace | Mustang, Oklahoma 73064 USA
1.888.361.9473 | www.tatepublishing.com

Tate Publishing is committed to excellence in the publishing industry. The company reflects the philosophy established by the founders, based on Psalm 68:11,
"The Lord gave the word and great was the company of those who published it."

Book design copyright © 2010 by Tate Publishing, LLC. All rights reserved.
Cover design by Kellie Southerland
Interior design by Stefanie Rooney

Published in the United States of America

ISBN:978-1-61663-742-2
1. Business & Economics, Leadership
2. Business & Economics, Management
10.07.21

Acknowledgement

This book, like my life, begins and ends with my beautiful wife, Kay. She was fifteen and I seventeen when we met on the sidelines of a football field. She was a cheerleader and I was a football player. Kay has never dropped her "pom poms" during our entire marriage. She has cheered me on through many difficult times and certainly during the writing of this book. Without her faith in me, without her love and passion, I can assure you this book would yet be a manuscript.

Jim Stovall. This book venture began over dinner one night when I was sharing my passion and Jim said, "You need to write a book." My first response was very reserved, but Jim dropped the seed that created this book. He is a remarkable human being, totally blind and yet achieving more than 100 sighted men all combined into one. One of my highest honors in life is to have Jim Stovall call me his mentor. Jim has also been blessed to have a perfect mate, his wife, Crystal.

Mr. Zig Ziglar. What can be said about a man who has contributed more to the substance of ethical leadership than any other public speaker? Knowing this man for many decades has been most memorable. His personal encouragement by his actions has been incredible over the years. His love for his wife, his commitment to Christ, and his belief in humanity have set the standard for all leaders.

John Maxwell. I first met John when I invited him to speak to a group of business leaders in California. His message about his grandson and hitting the ball has remained fresh in my mind: *"Just swing the bat."* It is especially meaningful now that I have a grandson in sports. There are hundreds of what I call "paper leadership teachers" around the world, meaning what they write looks good on paper, but in real life it flops. John is the real deal. No other man on this planet has mentored more leaders with such a high degree of success than John Maxwell. Like Zig and Jim, he is a man of character and passion put on earth to raise the bar of leadership for those who follow, a man who is not ashamed to give glory to God.

A special thanks for two incredible ladies. My personal assistant, Luda, who over the past decade has made sure I am at the correct place at the correct time for speaking and who read this manuscript endless times. Also to my personal editor, Linda. The lady who always makes me sound better in writing both my monthly articles and this book. To both of you ladies, thank you for your efforts and commitment.

Finally, how could I impart the attributes I find in leaders without acknowledging those I've led? A special thank you to the thousands who have been under my leadership over the past three decades. Mentioning every one would require its own book. You each know who you are and how we enjoyed a special journey together. Thank you for your loyalty, trust, and friendship; and I look forward to following your careers as you develop your leadership skills.

My life has been full following and knowing these people; I am blessed beyond all measure. Thank you, my love and my friends, for your dedication and purpose to serve others before yourselves.

"I live for Christ; I love my wife; I lead my kids and grandkids. Then I look for those who need to know that life offers more than just a living."

Bob Goshen

TABLE OF CONTENTS

Author's Note

Success or failure of organizations and corporations rests on one simple fact: either you have created leaders or you have no leaders. You can have all the passion, excitement, great ideas, and marvelous plans for expanding your business or organization, but without leaders who are capable of executing your vision, you will continually experience setbacks producing a higher overall risk of failure. You can possess the greatest business concept on earth— you might have created the perfect plan to expand your existing organization, you may feel that you have the finest product or service ever desired by men and women, but remember, no product or plan will move or succeed without people, and those people must have proper leadership with a single goal: creating more leaders.

"People move products; products do not move people."

Leadership is rare. It is difficult to find a person who has the skills to continually improve himself while mentoring others to be the best they can be. Many books have been written on leadership, scores of great men and women have penned marvelous words on the subject, and I am more than confident that many of the concepts I discuss in this book have been expounded on at one time or another. However, I have found in my lifetime that the manner in which something is related is as profound as the original thought. If you are a parent, think of the times when you told your kids something only to have them ignore the instruction, and then a guest speaker at school or church says exactly the same thing and you hear from their lips, "Wow, that was the greatest advice I have ever heard."

Simple explanation: they were not ready to hear the information at the time you shared it, but as life moved them along, they began to be more receptive. So it is in writing this book, I am hoping that many will be ready to receive the information.

I am sharing in this book what I have personally observed over thirty-three years of moving from employee to entrepreneur. I will share examples and stories that I am confident will give you tremendous insight on how to develop leaders. It was during this time that I changed my own personal business philosophy from a focus on marketing plans and products to the people I employed to assist in the execution of my vision. I discovered that developing a personal relationship with those under my leadership went beyond any pay raise or business plan. I learned that shareholder value had no value until I had created a team to execute the strategy.

The most prominent question I receive when I do leadership seminars is, "How do I follow someone who has no ability to lead?" The question doesn't surprise me. I have viewed firsthand men and women in areas of leadership who have no business leading. Today is the day to look into your corporations and organizations and ask if those who are in leadership have earned the trust and respect to lead. Are the proper principles being taught through your leadership team?

Defining Leadership
The Positive, Progressive, Ethical Influence on Others

Before I offer a personal definition of leadership, let me say that leadership is not a title or position. Many relate leadership to the initials behind a person's name, such as CEO, or to a position, such as president. Sadly, many say "I can never be a leader," but what they mean is I can never be a business owner, CEO, or president of a major college. I recently gave a keynote presentation followed by a three-hour session on leadership to the staff and professors at a major university. Many in attendance brought their mates to the dinner where I was speaking. Mothers of small children and ladies who were now grandmothers were in the audience. I received applause when I suggested that the most difficult position associated with leadership is being a mother. I now have grandchildren, and the privilege of baby-sitting them overnight has required me to apologize to my wife for years of taking her position for granted. No individual has a more meaningful role than a mother raising children. The job demands leadership skills in many cases way beyond those found in leaders of companies. As I share my definition of leadership, it is important to emphasize that the information I share relates to every individual, whether they have a title or not.

Leadership has been described as the process of social influence in which one person is able to enlist the aid and support of others in the accomplishment of a common task. However, a search of any local bookstore could easily produce more than 100 titles on leadership, each author offering a unique definition. I recently Googled the word leadership and received 163,000,000 hits. Although countless definitions can be found on the Internet, finding men and women who have actually taken an organization and expanded it by creating new leaders is very rare. We should not be impressed by college reviews or various polls and surveys taken on the subject; instead we need to look for actual examples of people who began with nothing and created leaders from followers.

Several years ago I invited John Maxwell to a meeting in Southern California where I was holding an event for the sole purpose of teaching leadership. I had invited 500 key business owners to this special event and asked John to share his wisdom. I admire John greatly because he is one of the few who has actually built a leadership team from the ground up and gone on to secure the team, walking the leadership walk.

During his outstanding address to my leadership team, he summarized the definition of leadership with one word: "influence." How simple and how true. A leader is one who simply influences the behavior of those around him in word and deed. I believe that definition is true, but I began to think about the evil men and women in leadership positions who influenced others. Hitler, Stalin, Jim Jones. And on any given day the newspapers disclose stories of men and women in leadership positions on Wall Street, in the political arena, or corporate America whose influence (while perhaps not evil) has been destructive. John's comments were absolutely true; analyze the equation and it really is all about influence. However, I would like to add to his definition and share how those in leadership should not only consider how to influence others but also the method in which they influence.

I define leadership as the "positive, progressive, ethical influence on others." Leaders should not only influence others, but they need to do it in such a way that it builds people up, encourages and edifies them so they can duplicate this attitude in others. The true measure of a leader is how well he or she mentors people so personal leadership is handed off to others to create new leaders. We are to develop others to continue when we are no longer around.

Positive

An effective leader is a positive leader. The question will always be, can a leader lead and not be positive? Yes, but after a few short years they will have no one left to lead. One only has to reflect on their personal journey in life to understand this principle. Remembering our feelings when our parents, a teacher, or boss was negative reminds us that we didn't want to be around that person. Second, we probably didn't listen to that person.

I will be the first to agree that it is very challenging to remain positive in such a negative world. Turning on the television at six p.m. makes us feel like our endorphins are departing from our bodies. Viewing murders, thefts, international conflicts, and political scandals makes it easy to believe the world is doomed for destruction the following day. Conversations at work are rarely uplifting and edifying. I am afraid to report that for the most part life becomes a daily soap opera on how people are failing in their finances, marriages, and the raising of their children. Even when we go to the movies it is rare to find something that comes from a positive position. And of course there is the daily drive to work, where some use sign language as a response to our driving habits. I think we can honestly say that the world around us is generally negative.

Leaders must be above negative circumstances. They must focus on the positive results they desire and not focus on the existing negative activities that surround them. A leader must become that one person everyone looks forward to being around, the person who offers simple solutions to everyday problems, the person who can light up the room when he or she enters. A leader must become the person who makes everyone else feel better about themselves. Their message must be simple and sincere, creating belief in those around them that their day will be better.

Today and every day, from the time you get up in the morning until you put your head on the pillow, you will influence ("lead") a minimum of twelve people. From your mate, to your kids, to fellow drivers in traffic, to employees, to your boss, you are constantly influencing others. Ask yourself: is my influence negative or positive?

Smash the Rearview Mirror

It is difficult to step up to the next level in life and become a leader if we are continually looking in the rearview mirror and focusing on negative aspects of our jobs, circumstances, or past failures. I can guarantee that I have had many setbacks in my life, and at those times I felt totally overwhelmed. But if we are to move ahead we must move on; we can't continue to reflect on past failures and expect to move our organization or our career forward.

When my son was young, I volunteered to assist his high school as a football coach. Because I played linebacker in college, they gave me the assignment of coaching linebackers. One young man was very impressive. He was 6′2″, weighed around 240 pounds, and was extremely physical. During practice he was the first on the field and the last one off, and along with his athletic ability came a 3.5 grade-point average. This young man would be considered a strong candidate for a collegiate football career.

However, he possessed one problem. If he missed a tackle, he would bring his negative attitude back to the huddle. Cursing and complaining, he would repeat, "I should have done this" or "I should have done that." And as the game progressed, he would become worse. It was a shame to see such a great athlete lose it so easily.

After a bad play during practice, I pulled him over to the side of the huddle, held his facemask, and made him look me in the eyes. I said, "Bill, there is not one young man on this field who has your skills. From your dedication to your work ethic, you excel. But, son, unless you learn how to leave the previous play behind you and look forward to the next play, you will never become a candidate for college football." From that day forward he began to cool off and understand that the "past was the past," and he owed it to his team and coaches to focus on the next play.

It is impossible to move forward and become positive if we refuse to leave the negative in the past. I have learned that 50% of folks really do not wish to hear my negative thoughts, and the other 50% are somewhat glad that whatever was negative happened to me. Drop the negative and forget about what has not worked in the past. Each day is a new start. Look at past negative failures as the finest educational moments of life. Move forward speaking positive energy for the future. When I think of positive speech, I'm reminded of three things: a boat, a horse, and a cigarette.

My wife and I just returned from a wonderful Mediterranean cruise that began and ended in Spain. The ship was the length of over five football fields and its weight over 40,000 tons. As we sailed home on our final night, we encountered twelve-foot waves and high winds. It was remarkable to think that the rudder, this hunk of iron, was the only thing controlling the direction of our ship.

I will never forget our beautiful, pure white Arabian stallion. He was an outstanding horse. However, he presented a challenge, especially to me. Each time I entered the barn, he would lay his ears back, snarl his gums, and flare his nostrils as if saying, "You want some of this?" Being the true horseman that I am, I did what any wise person would do: I called my wife. She was amazing. She would stand directly in front of him, tell him to "save it," and then proceed to put a lead rope around his neck and slip a tiny metal bit into his mouth. Astonishing. That tiny bit took 1600 pounds of fire and rage and turned him into an obedient horse.

Recently in our state we had the worst year for grass fires since 1920. At last count over 100,000 acres had been burned. It was reported in the news that a tiny stick weighing less than one ounce—a cigarette—had ignited the majority of the fires.

A small rudder can control direction; a small piece of metal can change a temperament; and a piece of paper weighing less than an ounce can cause thousands of acres of damage—and so it is with a very tiny part of our anatomy called the tongue. We have a choice as leaders to use the tongue to build up or tear down others, to create energy or exhaustion in our organization, to influence others positively or negatively. We as leaders know it is imperative we understand the power of our tongue.

How is it possible to create the habit of being positive rather than negative? It is a choice, and the following three steps can make the choice much easier.

1. Define your environment. Before your day begins, determine that you will escape negative influences when possible. If you are in a group of negative people, excuse yourself in a way that does not put them down but allows you a way of escape. More than once in my life I have said, "Please excuse me. I must go to the men's room," and often I never return. "Ooops, just remembered I have a phone call to make" is another easy out. It amazes me when I hear of a person who answers an obscene telephone call and stays on the line trying to discuss with the caller why he/she should not be engaged in such behavior. The caller only continues the profanity without taking a breath. I have always asked, "Why

do you stay on the line? Why not immediately hang up?" So it is with your environment. When people begin to spread negativity, think of it like an obscene phone call and just hang up by walking off. Either you will control your environment or others will do it for you. As a leader, it is imperative to establish an environment of optimism, a place where people want to be, a place where those you are leading feel safe and lifted up in their spirits.

2. Guard your mind. Negative television, negative music, negative books, and negative movies create negative people. We become what we watch and read. If you allow your mind to receive negative input, you have no choice but to produce negative output. It is like the person who says they wish to lose weight while they eat a double meat cheeseburger. Just as you become what you eat, you will become what you allow into your mind. Leadership demands the guarding of your mind; it demands you rise to a higher level of discernment of those things that will bring you down. Leaders guard their minds and monitor very closely those things they read and view.

3. Watch your words. Nothing annoys me more when I speak at a function than when, after my talk, a person comes up and says, "I'm just a housewife ... " "I'm just a car salesman ... " "I'm just a teacher ... " "I'm just a _____." This immediately tells me the person has work

to do in the area of self-confidence. No matter your occupation, be proud, and do not allow the words from your mouth to make you inferior to anyone. Kill the word "just" before you state your occupation, and see yourself being created as a unique individual.

As a leader, be very cautious with your choice of words when you mentor others. Your words should offer encouragement, not despair; they should edify people and build them up rather than put them down and damage their spirit. If any of your words are used to put others down in order to build yourself up, you are far from being a leader. A leader leads with positive words that result in positive actions. As Proverbs tells us, "Life and death are in the power of the tongue."

Doing the Right Thing in the Wrong Way

I will never forget the lessons I learned from people who tried to be positive in a negative way. It was my freshman year in college, and I was on the football team. Our college had done very poorly over the past few years, and we were in the locker room ready to go out on the field when we received the following pep talk from the head coach: "Gentlemen, they are bigger than we are; they are stronger than we are; they have more talent than we have; so let's go get 'em." Wow! I was really excited about going out of that dressing room and playing after that pep talk! We were beaten 66 to 6 on that autumn day, but it was not enough to disappoint our coach. Right after the game he brought us back to the dressing room to tell us, "Do not be disappointed; I somewhat expected this result today."

While I was attending college, I had a friend who lived next door to us who was a wrestler at the university. He and his wife purchased a small dog and knew that my wife, who owned a pet shop at the time, was well-versed regarding pets. So he brought his dog to my wife and asked how to housebreak the puppy. Kay told them to put paper in the kitchen, and when the puppy was about to do its thing simply correct the puppy with a soft pat on its rear and place it on the newspaper to accomplish its task. She told them to reinforce the puppy by saying "good dog" after he completed the project.

Two weeks later he came to us and said that his dog was not doing well. The dog was doing its thing in the living room and then running to the paper. Well, it seems my friend got the message a little backward. He would grab the dog when it began doing its business and say "good dog" as he picked it up and ran to the paper where he would give the dog a little swat. The lesson: know the proper place to reinforce good behavior.

A leader who establishes a positive environment will be the one who continually receives positive results.

Progressive

Will Rogers said, "Even if you're on the right track, you'll get run over if you just sit there." So it is in leadership. Leaders do not have the luxury of sitting around and waiting for results. I have a friend who is a billionaire. Recently, on his private jet to Spain, we were discussing business and his expectations. Now here is a man who has a 40,000-square-foot home, owns one of only two jets in its category in the world, a Rolls Royce limo, a manufacturing and distribution company that is the envy of the world, and everything he owns is paid for with cash. He averages five hours of sleep per night, just turned sixty years of age, and continues to seek better ideas and advice. He reads articles, he studies trends, and he seeks continual data and information. By many standards people would say he has done it all, but by his standard he believes he is just beginning.

True leaders never stop being students. If they feel they know it all and can no longer learn anything from others, arrogance has overwhelmed common sense, and pride will be the beginning of their fall.

I had a company that was quite successful in the sports industry. I sold products to virtually every high school and college in America. In conjunction with sales, I created brochures or banners that I placed in schools to expand my brand. One such creative piece showed a weight lifter, sweat running down his face, and every vein in his body bulging. Below the picture the statement read, "When you're not training, someone somewhere else is, and when you meet them they will win." In today's environment we do not have the luxury to read our press releases. It does not matter what our business or organization is doing now; it is what are we going to be doing tomorrow, the next day, and next year to serve more people and create more leaders. All great leaders share one commonality: after that final day of life on this earth, when the headstone is engraved, it will read, "If I just had one more minute."

Being progressive means not resting on past accomplishments. It is easy to get caught up in our own press, to create a sort of self-pride that allows us to believe we are better than others. A principled leader understands it is by God's grace he has created what he has, and it is by the same grace and favor that he will move forward.

As I mentioned, we have Arabian horses, and one thing we learned early in showing our horses was never to become what is called "barn blind," believing that the animal you own is better than it is. It is a tendency I have guarded against in myself (applied with some humor) when I speak to organizations. After an introduction that lists my accolades and accomplishments, I often begin by saying, "I wish my wife and kids were impressed with all of that."

Well-grounded leaders are the first to admit they are the product of those around them in the past or present who believed in them when others did not. They know that what their leadership has created is a gift, and with the gift comes a great deal of responsibility to help others.

Progressive leaders work on themselves before they work on others. They want to be that person who is always willing to serve and mentor those around them. They believe school is never out for them, and they are always working to become better in order to serve more people. Progressive leaders work to become better in all areas of life: mentally, physically, socially and spiritually. Progression is built into the nature of the leader, always seeking input on how to improve, seeking new knowledge, seeking the camaraderie of men and women of like mind.

Here are seven keys to staying progressive:

1. *Read.* I have found reading biographies to be very helpful. I was in the service during the Viet Nam War, and a statement used many times was, "If you are going through a mine field, follow someone and you will come home much taller." Many of the minefields in life can be avoided if we follow men and women who have accomplished more than we have. Some of my favorite books are about Mary Kay Ash, Sam Walton, Jack Welch, Lee Iacocca, Ronald Reagan, and General Patton. In addition to biographies, focus on books, articles, and publications related to your area of expertise. I have found great benefit in leadership books written by Zig Ziglar and John Maxwell. Subscribe to magazines that publish articles related to your endeavors. Leaders are often pressed for time, so keep a folder on your desk labeled "To Read." When you see an article that would add to your knowledge, clip it and put it in the folder. On your next business trip, put the folder in your briefcase and read the articles while you are flying. I don't have the luxury to read all the books I would like to that are related to my field, but

I found a great resource called *Executive Book Summaries*. In addition to sending you a book summary, they include a great outline, and they highlight the major points in the book. When you are reading in your hotel room or on an airplane, it is easy to get out your yellow marker and underscore information that relates to your business. I often will review eight to ten books on one trip.

2. *Subscribe.* I subscribe to *USA Today, The Wall Street Journal,* and my local newspaper to stay informed on current events and do a quick look at headlines that might affect my industry.

3. *Listen.* Leaders in every industry have recorded lectures or seminars on CDs or DVDs. Your professional association newspapers will often share what is available and where to order. You can also download much of this material from the Internet. Put it on your iPod so you can listen while you work out at the gym or in your drive time to work. Always keep a yellow pad on the passenger's seat ready to write down a thought that might assist in your personal development. Once again, flying time is a great time for listening.

4. *Network.* Joining a club or association in your area of expertise can add value to your ongoing knowledge. As a professional speaker, I belong to the National Speakers Association. Each month we have professional speakers from around the United States share their wisdom

on how to become a better speaker and expand our business. The value of having someone in your profession give you fresh input is priceless.

5. *Mentor.* Iron sharpens iron, and so it is with a mentor. Find someone who will offer you their time, perhaps over lunch or dinner, to guide and direct you. I have been blessed to have mentors in my life who have enriched my experience and knowledge. A good mentor reinforces your direction and can often see a potential problem that you do not see. As a leader, I also want to encourage you to be a mentor to someone who could benefit from your years of experience.

6. *Teach.* To stay sharp in your field, take some time to teach others. You can do this, as I stated above, by becoming a mentor. Giving sound advice keeps you current and reinforces your beliefs. You can do this one-on-one, or if you have the opportunity and ability to share with many, move out and do it. Relating to others what you have learned is not only rewarding but also refreshing.

7. *Journal.* Write your thoughts and ideas in a book, what worked and what did not work in your journey. Record what you hear from other leaders; there is something magical about moving ideas from your head to your hand. It helps you to internalize the information and allows you the ability to better express yourself as you incorporate your personal thoughts and personality into the information.

Ethical

Ethics: "A system of moral principles."

Ethics is the glue that holds a corporation or organization together. Sadly, its lack or loss has become the number one topic during the past several years.

From scandals on Wall Street to those holding public trust in Washington D.C., the lack of ethics has been the fall of many. Ethics is the one element that separates a mere person of influence from a leader with major influence. It's that spirit within the person that continually questions, "Is this right? Will what I do help or hurt people? Will my actions create a potential conflict of interest? Will my action bring shame to my friends and family? How will this decision affect my board members and shareholders? How will this action affect my organization?" We must teach and train our up-and-coming leaders to ask these questions, and they must sift their thoughts through this grid when they serve others.

Every leader is always fewer than three "lights" away from making unethical decisions that can destroy their leadership position. From this day forward, let every intersection with a traffic light be a lesson in ethical decision making, consider my three light example, the green light, the yellow light, and the red light. Leaders should lead thinking ahead just as a driver must when entering an intersection. Any question related to an ethical decision should always "get a green light." However, when making decisions we often find ourselves in the middle of the intersection and under the influence of the yellow light; at that crucial deciding moment we still have the option to stop or continue. We can proceed with a decision that may compromise our character, or we can simply say NO; we can stop at the red light. None of us is immune. Each day, those of us in leadership are put into situations that will challenge our ethics. Because this is undeniable, the leader must get up each morning already having decided how he or she will respond to those moments of character challenges.

Ethics must be key in the mission statement and corporate culture developed by the leader. Ethics underscores fairness in decision-making. Ethics drives the leader to even deeper questions, such as: "How will this decision affect the welfare of those who are under my leadership? Will this decision help or hurt the morale of those I am leading?" Often, those in the position of leadership make a decision based on how it will affect the organization's growth rather than how it will affect those who contribute to the organization's growth. When decisions are made from a "command and control" mindset rather than collaborating with the people who will be affected, a "cultural barrier" is created that prevents progress.

We have been sold a story line that "life isn't fair." Well, for some things this may hold true, as in the case of weather or accidental fires. But for those of us who have been given the privilege of leading others, all decisions that can affect the livelihood of the people in our organizations must pass the test of "Will this help or hurt the relationships within my organization? Will the decision I make create a question of conflict of interest?" (Note: Not "Will it create a conflict," but

"Will it create a *question* of conflict?") Each decision must be made considering the ethical consequences and how this decision will affect those you lead. Will the decision violate their trust? Will the decision have the potential of hurting those who have placed their trust in my leadership?

Trust is continually in the balance when leading others. Companies and organizations have come to a complete standstill due to trust being violated. Just as a marriage is built on trust, so it is with organizations. Trust is the baseline for ethics, and once it is violated it is virtually impossible to restore it. It immediately drives people in the organization to look for other opportunities in organizations where they feel trust can be reestablished. Here are ten actions that can violate trust:

1. Making decisions related to bottom-line profit before considering how it will affect those in your organization. Decisions based on profit instead of principles.

2. Becoming arrogant, believing that you and only you are capable of all the answers. Pride does precede the fall of man.

3. Hiring or placing people in your organization in high-profile positions without communicating with those on your existing leadership team that might be capable.

4. Taking away benefits that have long been in place without lengthy communication and explanation with those it will affect.

5. Promoting family members or others as a result of favoritism rather than proven performance.

6. Putting additional responsibility and work on people without adding an increase in income or reward.

7. Creating a negative environment by placing demands and compulsory rules on people.

8. Making changes in a marketing plan without consulting with those who will be expected to execute the change.

9. Creating an organization or corporation that is run by "centralization of power" instead of "decentralization of power."

10. Creating an environment where those under your leadership feel they are no longer of value.

It only takes a few of these actions to violate trust in an organization or corporation. We must build this mantra into our culture and most importantly into our potential leaders: Ethics is the glue that holds the organization together. Once those in leadership or ownership of a corporation begin making decisions based on profits rather than ethics and moral values, the momentum required to move an organization forward is immediately curtailed, and the paradigm switch begins. The entity leaves the area of excitement and creativity and is relegated to the internal battles that cause confusion and ultimately take the life from the organization.

We often find the biggest battle for growth and expansion never lies in the competition but rather within the halls and walls of a company that lost its moral compass. When we take a hard look at any failure or confusion in an organization and work to discover how it happened, we have to look no further than the ethical values of the leadership. Power placed in the hands of people without ethics is power that will always fail. It is no longer shocking how often leaders shoot themselves in the foot—but it is amazing how fast they reload the gun and do it again.

No One is Immune

As leaders we must never say, "I would never do that." As we look at the financial landscape today and the decisions made without ethical standards, and even as we look at the religious community, we see that great men and women have made decisions based on profit rather than ethics. We must realize that each of us has the capacity to fall into the trap of making decisions that are not ethical.

I would suggest that the majority of people in prison for making unethical decisions were good folks who never woke up in the morning saying, "How can I harm people?" It is a slow process for most, often beginning with an absence of guidance or in ignoring the value of a mentor with strong ethical values. It often begins in a person who starts with little and through hard work and commitment has built a business or organization that excels. Then they begin surrounding themselves with "yes" people, those who will never challenge their thinking or decisions. Next they develop a major memory lapse; they forget those who were there to assist them along their way to fortune or success. They actually begin to believe they have arrived at their destination only because of their personal wisdom and the gifts bestowed on them as if they were some sort of special human. Finally, they make all of their decisions based on what they think, not on what is ethical. Their decision-making moves toward the path of superiority in thinking. Having abandoned those who were there for them in the early years, they justify the abandonment by believing those folks no longer have value, that those folks are not as smart as they have become.

Once a person in leadership begins to isolate himself from those who offer differing ideas based on logic and ethics, the road moves from upward to downward. Whether you are a high-profile entertainer, the pastor of a mega church, a politician, CEO, or leader of an organization, you must allow others to hold you accountable.

How to Stay on an Ethical Track

Mentorship is the number one requirement for a leader. But a mentor must be chosen based on their character and ethics rather than their knowledge in a particular field of endeavor, a man or woman who is successful and bases that success upon the fair treatment of those they lead. Remember the words, "Those who associate with the wise will remain wise." Ethics keep us grounded as we progress in success. We must find that person or persons who will keep our feet to the fire, who we can respect enough to allow them to hold us accountable.

Staying on that ethical track means that we hold ourselves stable by not moving from the position of confidence to the position of arrogance. We can't give a lot of thought to the press we receive. In a recent interview with Brooks and Dunn after they won their seventh or eighth Grammy award, they simply said, "We have yet to impress ourselves." When narcissism moves in, rational thinking moves out.

It helps to keep that library of biographies current, those stories of men and women who created long-term success in an ethical manner. Sure, no one is perfect; the only perfect person was crucified on a tree. But books abound recounting the experiences of men and women who kept their lives together while experiencing phenomenal success. There are great examples all the way from biblical characters to current leaders who lived ethically and operated from a position of servanthood.

Outstanding organizations generate huge profits without allowing their profit to divert them from their central purpose and ethics. As the leader of an existing organization, one who is working to build leaders, continue down the path of those ethical corporations and set core values always based on serving others first.

Each day work to be positive, remain constant in personal development, and keep the corporate culture alive that has ethics as the centerpiece. Begin each morning remembering that leadership is a gift, never to be abused. If you implement these principles, you will have a major influence on those you have been given to lead.

Creating a Leadership Environment

People Move Products. Products
Do Not Move People. So You
Must Get the People Right.

Success comes at a much greater rate when you understand the principle that all of your success is based on those you lead. Sure, you can offer a great product and have the finest idea of the ages, but if you do not know how to orchestrate your leadership to perform, all is in vain.

As I mentioned, during my college years I was fortunate enough to play football. I wish I could say our team went to several bowl games and won the national title, but during my tenure our record was horrible. Consider this, we had the worst record in college football, but the following year, when many of the seniors were graduating, we placed ten players in the National Football League, all of whom became starters their first year and had outstanding careers in the NFL.

Think about what I just shared. Ten players were on the same team as starters on a college team with a miserable win/loss record, but they became stars in the NFL. Why?

In my opinion, the college coach was more focused on how the team would look each week and how often to change the playbook. He focused more on the playbook than the players. Once the players moved into the NFL, the coaches focused more on the players, getting them to believe they were capable of executing the plays developed by the coaches. The emphasis was on the *person* rather than the *plays*.

No One Can Perform Beyond the Way He Sees Himself

Organizations and corporations are losing leaders at a record rate because they don't understand this simple principle. For years I was the one who put all focus on the bottom line—profit—and overlooked the fact that those I was leading created my bottom-line profit. What a wake-up call! That is why I am so determined to get the message to leaders that *when you get the person right, the business grows*.

Your endless endeavor as a leader is to continually build the self-esteem of those you lead. Do not fall into the trap of believing your intelligence, product, or service is substantial enough to create continued growth. Look to those you rely on to move that product or service and work continually to create an environment that allows their optimal growth.

Let's look at two outstanding companies as an example. Southwest Airlines has created a corporate culture demonstrating to their employees that they are number one. They continually reinforce this message—daily, weekly, monthly, and yearly. And they do not hesitate to credit their success to the performance of their people. The proof that this philosophy makes a difference can be found in the profit sheets of the other airlines. The second company is the Marriott hotels. I had the opportunity to serve on a committee with Bill Marriott Jr. Visit with him, and it won't take long to realize he places all of his success in his people. He has created such a trust with his employees that they are willing to do almost anything to assist Mr. Marriott to succeed. He has a very open policy with his employees. He has created a 24-hour hotline so any employee who has a personal or financial challenge can receive immediate help. Mr. Marriott believes if he can assist his employees at their point of need, they will make better employees by not bringing those challenges to work, thus focusing on the needs of their hotel guests. Every person who has been placed in a position of leadership should read his book, *The Spirit to Serve*. (Unfortunately, the book is no longer in print. If you are unable to locate a copy, contact my office. I have some on hand.)

Performance is based on self-esteem. Those we are leading struggle each day based on their past or current failures. They do not feel confident due to this baggage, a past divorce, financial failure, family challenges with children or mate, or physical challenges. They have a problem cutting loose the chains of these past or current failures. These folks are everywhere in our organizations. These are the folks we rely on to execute our marketing and business plan. These are the folks who serve our clients daily on a one-on-one basis. Sometimes we give them the tools and instructions, but they just don't seem to move forward. My questions to you, the leader, would be: "How often have you sat down and listened to their needs? What do you know about them personally? Are they married or single? Do they have children or grandchildren? What role do they play in your organization?"

I go to Budapest, Hungary, a couple of times a year and always stay at the Marriott hotel. Last time I asked the restaurant manager to sit and share a cup of coffee with me. I informed him that I knew Bill Marriott Jr. and asked if he had ever met him. I was shocked to hear him say, "Several times." He told me Mr. Marriott would often drop into his hotels to visit the staff and answer any questions. He pointed to a corner of the restaurant and continued by saying, "Just a few short weeks ago Mr. Marriott asked that I bring all my waiters and chefs to the restaurant before it opened. He had us circle our chairs around him as he asked how we were doing, first with our families and then our jobs. He was very open and sincere."

And then he said he was shocked when Mr. Marriott would occasionally use the first names of some of his employees who had been at the hotel for some time, especially since they were not wearing nametags.

How long has it been since you have had such a relaxing conversation with those under your leadership? Now do you see why the performance rating of Marriott hotels is outstanding? Get the people right and performance is an automatic byproduct.

A dear friend and one of my mentors is Zig Ziglar. Several years ago we were visiting on the telephone and he indicated his desire to meet Jack Kemp. At that time Jack was the director of HUD in the White House. I informed Zig that I knew Jack and would be happy to make the introduction. A couple of days later I flew to Dallas where I met Zig, and we began our flight to Washington.

The opportunity to spend several hours with Zig was very memorable. I had read every book Zig had written. I had attended many events where Zig was speaking and heard him say his signature line many times, "You can have everything in life you want if you will just help enough other people get what they want." I heard it and I accepted it, but like many, I allowed it to roll off somewhere into my subconscious. However, it became personalized when during our discussion he looked at me and said, "Bob, continue helping people achieve their needs and your needs will be met."

The message is simple: Help people become better by helping them feel better about themselves. Once people raise their self-esteem they raise their self-awareness; they will believe that they are capable of doing better in this life. Help people take control of their fears and replace them with faith. Zig Ziglar has been billed over the past several decades as a motivational speaker, but when people say that I quickly make a correction by saying he is more than a motivational speaker, he is a "motivational teacher," and as leaders and managers it is our responsibility to produce and mentor as many "motivational teachers" as possible. These are the people who will move our organizations forward.

Leadership is Recovery So Get a GRIP

Leaders are like emergency room doctors—they are consistently in the action of recovery. We make our plans, create the team, and supply the vision and passion, and Bingo! That which we did not plan for has put itself front and center. A leader will soon learn that each day is spent in recovery. During the course of a day, the leader will have more challenges than most people will have in a month. What is their secret for being strong and effective? *Quicker recovery.* It is essential to move an organization toward its goals. It is my personal belief that what separates leaders from followers is the ability to prepare for challenges and create solutions. Followers seem to run from challenges where leaders understand challenges will come, and they look for solutions. They become Doctors of Solutions.

As you step up into leadership, simply learn to *get a GRIP.*

G = *Get ready* to recover daily; don't let failure take you by surprise. Prepare yourself mentally by not allowing external circumstances to control your internal commitment. Externally, things may look bad, but leadership is based on the internal not the external. Your internal principles must overcome what you hear and what you see.

R = Respond, don't react. Relax and use your reasoning skills. Do not allow yourself a knee-jerk reaction to the challenge. Prior to receiving my instrument rating, I found myself with a very challenging task. I was flying to Arkansas in a single-engine plane when I saw clouds approaching. Even though I was instructed not to fly above clouds given that I didn't have an instrument rating, I violated that principle and began to climb. As I approached 12,000 feet, it was evident I could not get above the clouds. I looked over at my young son and saw him begin to have breathing problems since our plane was not pressurized. I knew then that I had to breathe slowly and return to a fundamental of my flight training: "fly the plane first." I kept the wings level, fortunately found an opening in the clouds, and began to spiral through to get below them. To this day my son reminds me of that time in the sky. When we respond rather than react, we must immediately go back to basics, the principles that will put us back on a solid footing.

I = Initiate an immediate positive attitude. Recognize something good is going to come from this challenge. It is our natural state of mind when confronted with an obstacle to lean toward fear and the negative. I think of the patient who receives a negative medical report; the brain immediately thinks of "death" rather than "life." The body breaks out in a cold sweat as they begin to envision all the negative things that will come from this challenge. Train your mind each day to switch to the positive, for when you remain positive you remain in the area of creativity, and your brain begins to look for solutions. If we move to fear and doubt our brain begins to look at failure and defeat.

P = Prepare. During my time in the Navy, I was a spy. It was my task to locate and listen to our enemy as they sent out intelligence messages. As you can imagine, it was very exciting with each day bringing new challenges. Since those in our group were all given top priority clearances, we would continually prepare in case we were overrun by the enemy. Our plan included what we would do and how much time we had to get it done. We were to have this plan memorized so there would be no need to think about it; we could just do it. So it is in recovery; have a plan. Do not let tomorrow's challenges and negative attacks control you. Be ahead of the game by being prepared.

Leaders Create the Environment

We are told each day by CNN, Fox News, CBS, NBC, ABC, and others that the environment of our earth is in peril. Instead of taking a side on this issue, I would prefer to talk about another environment which, without proper discipline, will also become toxic, and that is the environment of the organization you are leading.

As leaders we can't change people, but we can create an environment that allows them to grow. The following ten elements should be considered when creating such an environment:

1. Depending on the size of your organization, create a website that will support those you are leading. Post the next meeting time for the staff or divisions of your organization, a calendar of company events that you would like to have your people attend, and any potential changes in marketing plans or activities that would affect employees' personal income or position as related to the management team.

2. Give your employees 24/7 email access to you. Allow them to communicate with you directly; discourage a "thirty-page document," but encourage them to present any challenges or areas they see that might improve operations. It is amazing how few will use this, but knowing they have the option is very important.

3. Meet with your key leaders a minimum of twice a year in a fun location. It might be a cruise or resort where they can leave the day-to-day challenges behind and enjoy some fun and fellowship. Encourage the involvement of their mate and kids. Relationships are created during these special times.

4. In addition, create a conference call to touch base and communicate on a regular basis. Where there is no communication there is potential for rumors.

5. Create a company ezine. Each month send everyone a one-page email sharing your vision and how important each person is to the overall success of the organization.

6. When possible, have random "fireside chats" with your people. Just arrive, pull up a chair, and have your folks gather around just to share and laugh.

7. Listen. When people you lead feel you are no longer listening to them, they move to the belief that they no longer offer value. When they feel they have no further value, they lose their passion for what they are doing and begin going through the motions rather than fulfilling a mission.

8. Have an open forum giving your people the opportunity to share how they feel about your leadership and the direction of the organization.

9. Never forget that people want to belong and that recognition can mean more than a pay raise. Pat them on the back, especially in front of their peers, if they do a great job. Building others up creates confidence, and where confidence prevails, performance will follow.

10. Believe in them.

The last in the list deserves further comment. I have often been asked how I have been able to take ordinary people and create outstanding leaders. There is no magic in the answer; it is simply supplying "belief transfer."

In the late 1970s I had a computing company. I was going to expand my product line by adding word processors, and the Fortune 100 company that would supply the products invited me to observe the interviews of potential sales people for the new product line. They were a large New York company with offices on Park Avenue. They wanted to show me the proper way to interview and find great talent, so they sent their key person in human resources to interview the candidates that would eventually work for me. My job was simply to sit and observe the master in action.

He interviewed scores of candidates, none of whom seemed impressive, and although it was nearing the end of the day, we agreed to one more interview. The young lady walked in. Her hair had been bleached to the point that it looked like straw, and her makeup was just not flattering. Her wardrobe was not coordinated, and her teeth were extremely crooked. When she entered the room, the person from New York smirked and slid her application over to me.

He quickly sent her on her way as he laughed, commented on how she looked, and questioned why she would even consider working in sales. This was on Friday, and we were to resume the interviews the following Monday.

I hurried home, and after dinner I opened my briefcase only to have this application fall out onto the table. I thought it had been thrown into the trash, but apparently I had slipped it into my briefcase. For some strange reason I thought I would take a quick look. I immediately contacted the human resources person from New York and informed him he could catch the next flight out because I was going to hire that last candidate. He broke out in laughter and began telling me there was no way she would last and she would be an embarrassment to my company. I could hear the sarcasm in his voice, and I am sure he went back to his Park Avenue office with stories about what a hillbilly I was and the woman with the Phyllis Diller hair.

The following day, I asked the young woman to meet me for coffee. She drove up to the coffeehouse in a car that matched her appearance—sort of a wreck. As she sat down, I asked a simple question: would she be willing to listen to instruction if it would offer benefit? Her answer was "Sure."

Over the next few weeks, I began to tell her how great she would be at her new job and how the clients would be so impressed with her knowledge. I sent her to a modeling school, to a top hair and makeup person, and to a dentist to repair her teeth. I began feeding her tapes and books on self-image and coached her on communications skills, and my wife spent additional time with her just sharing thoughts about life. I advanced her enough money for a new wardrobe and I leased a new car for her.

In less than five weeks I saw a person reinvent herself from the inside out. And in less than three years this young lady became the company's number one salesperson, not only in Oklahoma but in the entire United States. How did this occur? Belief transfer.

People must have someone believe in them when they cannot believe in themselves. I simply put her in an environment that offered total reinforcement of her self-esteem. You might ask "How did you know she would achieve such success?" Her resume (that the human resource person from New York hadn't read) stated that she was the word processing manager at a leading insurance company where she supervised more than twenty people who used IBM word processors. In addition, she was recently divorced and left with a young son. Our number one competitor was IBM, and the fact that she was recently divorced told me she needed to step up and make it happen for herself and her son. You see, my friends, get the person right and the future is bright. Every leader holds in his or her possession the greatest leadership tool on earth—*transferring their belief into others.*

The belief transfer process is key in the development of people, and especially leaders. The concept supports the understanding that the biggest challenge for any organization is the execution of a project or set of goals. From developing people to sharing a concept or a plan to establishing a strong customer service department, the process remains the same. If we are to get maximum results we must raise the self-image of the people we lead. Here's how we do this:

1. Focus on the good not the bad in a person.

2. See the person as you want them to be instead of how they are now.

3. Reinforce their value; let them know how important they are to the process.

4. Allow them to be a part of internal meetings that will affect the outcome of the organization.

5. Ask for their input and comments.

6. Give them responsibilities that demand they step up in leadership.

7. Take some time to play golf with them or some other activity they enjoy.

8. Communicate. Give them random phone calls to see how they are progressing.

9. Find out some personal details, kids, hobbies, etc.

10. Have faith in the person.

Family Unit

We all come from varied family backgrounds, some with no father or mother, some from broken homes, and hopefully some from in-tact family units. Being married for forty-four years and having three out-standing children and four perfect grandchildren gives me the ultimate leadership task, being a hus-band, a father, and a grandfather. Understanding the needs within a family unit and working to implement the same principles with those we lead makes our task extremely rewarding. The characteristics we must establish in order to lead others are not unlike those every child needs in a home environment.

Can those you are leading *trust* you? Do they believe you are honest and that you work with integr-rity? Do you respect those who have been assigned to your leadership? Do they understand how much you care about their success both at work and at home? Do you show them *compassionate* care? Do they see you not only as a leader but as a friend who is concerned about their future?

Those under your leadership must feel *stability*. They must sense that you have a handle on the future and that you are strong when tough decisions must be made. And the most important, in my personal opinion, is what I defined as belief transfer or *hope*. You must continually send the message that the future is bright. Even when things seem to be going south, you must remain focused on true north. Trust, compassion, stability, hope, these four words become the core for leading others. I remained true to these four building blocks as I personally led 150,000 people over a twelve-year period. I have witnessed ordinary people becoming super leaders using these principles. I have witnessed leaders creating additional leaders and growing overall performance as much as 35%.

It matters not if you are a father, mother, CEO, pastor, or founder and president of a company. If you wish for harmony and progress in any organization, you must first believe that your greatest asset is the people you lead. You must believe in them until they have the capacity to believe in themselves. They must believe they add value to the family unit or organization; they must be edified and uplifted on a regular basis, and they should always feel their input is valuable. So simple is this truth, but it is so undervalued in the world of leadership. Sadly, many people in the role of leadership are still using the obsolete command and control method.

Focus on people first, not marketing plans or products, and you will not only create growth but also secure it.

Discovering Leaders
Finding Diamonds in the Coal

A big question is "Where do you find leaders?" Wouldn't it be great to Google the word "leaders" and get thousands of names of proven leaders? How about if we could go to the yellow pages in our phone book and look up "proven leaders"? How about a little black book with endless names and phone numbers of qualified leaders by job description? Or a jobs category in the local newspaper's classified section with the heading "Leader." What if the doctor, upon delivery, pulled the newborn baby out, slapped it on the butt, and said, "Congratulations, Mrs. Jones, you have a nine-pound leader." I wish it were that easy, and who wouldn't agree? There is a great shortage of real leaders, men and women who have that servant heart and the ability to reason logically.

I do not believe we can actually discover leaders; I have found that leaders will discover us if we create the correct example and support system. If we set up a system that promotes people by their achievement and ability to help others achieve, leaders will be found. Leaders love to be around other leaders. They covet a relationship with people who know where they are headed and have a plan for how to get to their destination. So where can potential leaders be found? How do we recognize a potential leader?

Today we are seeing a mass exodus from corporate America, men and women who have simply had enough of the bureaucratic leadership that focuses on profits at the expense of people. Here is the sad truth: those who most often walk away are the leaders.

Let me share a very good example. I was recently visiting with a very sharp engineer who was hired by a Fortune 100 company. He was given a base salary in the $120,000 range and the possibility of an annual bonus of $100,000 to $200,000 more. In our conversation, he made it clear that he wants out of his job. He is waiting for the annual bonus and will then most likely say goodbye. Listen to his reasoning: "The environment is extremely demanding. They have just assigned me three additional responsibilities without any additional income or explanation of their expectations." He learned that a colleague was being paid more money and was contributing less, while he had just increased projected sales in his department from six million to seventeen million dollars with no recognition from those in leadership above him.

Now here is a young man who possesses the talent, has proven his value by consistently setting sales records, has been loyal, and most importantly is a self-governed person who requires very little oversight. Here is a person who possesses many of the skills I describe to be mentored into a leadership position, but he has in a very simple way been "abused" by the corporate system and a leadership that once again focuses on bottom-line profit rather than the importance of those who created the profits.

So once again a company sends out their best talent either to begin their own business or become a competitor only because they did not focus on the people. He is but one of many thousands who will depart their organizations this year because of a failure to understand the significance of the person rather than the plan.

Finding leaders within an existing environment can be easy if we are sensitive to the characteristics that define a leader. Unfortunately, people do not hang signs around their necks listing their leadership qualities, so we who are leaders must look for the invisible signs.

Common Characteristics of
an Effective Leader

Loyalty. You have those in your organization who have been loyal for years, working beyond what is required to support your corporate or organizational goals. They show up on time, work well with others, and create a positive bottom-line performance. They often take their work so seriously that they take it home, taking time from their mate and children.

Self-governance. They need very little if any oversight. You give them a project and they not only get the project done but also add additional value. They find the project as a challenge to their intellect and want to prove to themselves and to those who lead them that they have the capacity to add value to any project. Such a person is rare and once located should be mentored to even higher standards.

Belief in their ability to perform. When given a project, a potential leader feels confident that he or she can perform and satisfy all the requirements needed to accomplish the task. Their self-assurance stands out as they progress in determining how to attack the task at hand for the best results.

Play well with others in the sandbox. They have proven they can work with the people in their environment who have different values and leadership skills. They learn how to adapt to the environment they have been given and offer harmony instead of confusion and conflict.

Hunger to learn. They continually seek information and ask questions. They desire to learn as much as they can about the tasks they have been assigned. During meetings or conference calls they are the ones who ask deeper questions about a project or a proposal. These are a few of the qualities that can be found in those ready to become leaders. Some may possess only two or three of the characteristics, but they are ready to be groomed and mentored to increase their leadership skills.

The problem for most companies is that layers of bureaucratic people who are not leaders have been placed in positions of leadership, and they often overlook the person I have described. Or a worse scenario exists, the potential leader is seen as a threat to their immediate manager or supervisor, and therefore their name never comes up for advancement.

We as leaders must continue to create the environment where this cannot happen, for if it does, our best people will move on to either create their own business or go to a competitor who recognizes their value. It is because of this oversight of talent that organizations and corporations suffer today.

As I have flown more than four million air miles, I have met hundreds of new people. Approximately fifteen years ago I met a gentleman on a flight—a consultant—who gave me what he referred to as a "reverse evaluation"—a series of questions and answers used to evaluate leadership skills. Over the years, I have found his list to be very helpful in aligning the correct people with the correct positions, and I have used the evaluation in many companies and organizations with outstanding success.

The questionnaire is given to employees who answer questions related to their department leader or supervisor. There are no names attached to the questions, so the employee has the freedom to answer without any possible negative consequences. The purpose is to examine the leadership skills of the supervisor or manager and then to assist that person in improving the areas where they show to be weak. Using a scale of 1–5 with 5 being highest, each employee scores their immediate supervisor or manager.

1. Gives me freedom to accomplish goals
2. Allows me to participate in decision-making process
3. Teaches as opposed to giving orders
4. Listens, allows me to work out problems on my own
5. Confronts sooner rather than later
6. Is direct but not blameful, focuses on issues
7. Hears my side of the story
8. If my manager is wrong, will admit it
9. I know what I am supposed to do
10. There are no surprises at evaluation time
11. Feedback is done on a regular basis
12. Able to keep track of my progress because job is clearly defined
13. Able to take part in planning my job expectations

14. Hears all sides of conflicts

15. Allows me to participate in conflict-solving process

16. Even if I don't agree 100% with decision, able to speak my mind

17. Team meets regularly

18. Time is well spent

19. Can speak freely without fear

20. Manager makes effort to hear what I say

21. Positive recognition is consistent

22. Does not play "favorites"

23. Encouragement outweighs negative feedback

24. Makes extra effort to notice when I do well

25. Eliminates attitude of superiority

26. Works directly with me when necessary

27. Balances between being a leader (in charge) and a team member

28. Can count on his/her word

29. Does not take advantage of me

30. Sets standards of honesty and fair play

The questions are related to specific leadership skills, and when the evaluations are scored, critical strengths and weaknesses are revealed in the manager or supervisor's leadership ability. The questions all relate to the following characteristics:

1. *Confronting.* Confronts performance problems quickly and directly in a non-blameful and non-coercive way. Has flexibility to adjust and hear other side of the story.

2. *Establishing Task Clarity.* Makes sure each job is explicitly clear and performance evaluation is fair and directly related to job expectations.

3. *Resolving Disagreements and Conflicts.* Solves most conflicts so that no one feels like they have lost and all feel like they were treated fairly.

4. *Conducting Meetings.* Conducts meetings on an on-going basis and they are not considered a waste of time.

5. *Affirming Performance.* Makes a consistent and evenly distributed effort to recognize and acknowledge when employees do things well.

6. *Reducing Status Barrier.* Eliminates status barrier and any traces of superiority between him/herself and team members.

7. *Modeling Integrity and Honesty.* Establishes an environment of honesty and fair play between manager and team members, mostly by personal example.

8. *Facilitating.* Is changing from an order giver and controller of people to coach, team builder, and mentor. Allows team members the freedom and flexibility to solve problems and achieve goals on their own.

As leaders we must ask ourselves daily, do we shine in all eight characteristics? If not, then we are not serving those who depend on our leadership. As the head of a department or organization we should make it a goal to spend time looking for those who have the ability not only to understand our vision but add to the vision with additional thoughts and actions.

There is a direct correlation between leadership and the growth of an organization. The organization or corporation that will put its focus on people over profit and projects will sustain a much longer life.

A Leadership Lesson from a Master

While having dinner on the Presidential Yacht, *Sequoia*, in Washington, DC, I had the opportunity to have a conversation with a fellow committee member, Bill Marriott Jr. I asked him the secret to his success in finding the best general managers for his hotels. I anticipated an in-depth explanation. Perhaps he used a reverse evaluation to determine how each manager worked with his staff. Perhaps he employed a test that was an industry standard for hotel managers. Perhaps he simply looked for great candidates at competing hotels.

His reply was simply, "When I visit each hotel, I get the general manager and take him or her to the *heart of the house*. This term is used to describe the center of all activity—housekeeping and bookkeeping, reservations, and all other key departments in the hotel. It is the focal point or nerve center of the hotel. As I walk with the GM I take careful notice of how he or she is greeted. If the staff walks up with a smile, looking forward to seeing the manager, this is a great sign. If, on the other hand, I see no smile and very little eye contact, I am certain we have a potential challenge."

Isn't it interesting that a key indicator of the success of Marriott's general managers is not their years of experience in another hotel, nor their grade point average in hotel and restaurant management, but how they relate to those they lead? It is what I refer to as their "people skills." A great leader is one who can create relationships with those given to him or her for mentorship.

How many corporations or organizations reduce their performance and often their bottom line because they have people who lack "people skills" in leadership positions? An organization is a reflection of its leadership.

While staying at the Marriott in Budapest, Hungary, I asked one of the managers, "Can you see the continuation of Bill Marriott and his leadership principles being carried out by your management staff here in Budapest? Since Mr. Marriott is the head and he is thousands of miles from this hotel, do you see his corporate culture carried out consistently?"

The manager answered with a story relevant to Hungary. "When you go to the fish market to buy a fish, you should always smell the head. If the head stinks, the entire fish is bad." So it is in leadership. If the head of the company or organization "smells," it is likely the entire company or organization is dead.

Every corporation needs a *heart of the house*, a place where leaders can meet with those they lead to inspire, encourage, and mentor.

Duplicating Leaders
Mentorship that Measures

When it was revealed that Steve Jobs of Apple Computer would be stepping down for a period of six months to face health challenges, the announcement brought Apple stock prices down more than 5%. Why? Apple has done an excellent job creating one of the finest products in the world; I am currently typing this manuscript on their latest computer. Their invention of the iPod, the iPhone, and the iPad has changed how we manage music, visual and printed media, gaming, and telephone communications. Years of research and development have been focused on products and marketing schemes that have created, to this date, a healthy bottom-line profit for Apple.

So why the drop in stock? While it may be true that Mr. Jobs has a succession plan in effect, it was not introduced on the day they released the challenging news that he was stepping aside. It appears that Apple had spent more time concentrating on products rather than people. This brings up the next step in leadership, and that is not only finding leaders but also *duplicating leaders.* For if a company desires to have long-standing success and the security of continued growth, they must not only create leaders but they must go to the next step, which is to duplicate leadership in the organization—creating what I refer to as "Layered Leadership."

This can only be accomplished by creating a corporate culture where the head of the organization continually sends the message that success is not measured in "bottom-line profits" or "shareholder value" but rather in how many leaders can be created in the corporate environment. If an organization looks at duplicating leadership, not only will personal performance be off the charts, but those results being sought will come faster.

Mentorship that Measures

The measure of a corporate culture is whether new leaders are being duplicated through a mentorship program. Those who have become leaders must be responsible to coach new leaders. As related previously, they must first locate the leader and then be certain they have established the environment to support the person's growth. Leaders within an organization or corporation might feel this process is somewhat futile, since they are mentoring people who could possibly be their replacement.

Let me offer a great deal of comfort. If you have the ability to locate and mentor people to leadership positions, your value has just increased greatly within the organization you represent, and if that value is not recognized and appreciated, rest assured there are thousands of organizations and corporations desiring someone with that ability. The most needed asset in any organization is leadership. It is a quality that organizations search for on a daily basis, and anyone with that ability possesses a skill that will be highly valued.

It matters not if you are a mother, father, CEO, college president, or pastor, you must look toward the future and continually ask, "How am I establishing leadership traits in those for whom I am responsible? Have I established the proper corporate culture to edify those in my organization who create additional leaders?"

See it, Do it, Teach it

I was watching a documentary on television showing how the critical care emergency facility in a Chicago hospital responded to emergencies. During a twelve-hour shift they see everything from fatal car accidents to gunshots and burns. In addition to treating those

coming to the facility, they also use this time to train
new doctors. As a person entered the emergency room
with a major gunshot wound, the camera was rolling
while the commentator began to ask questions. "How
do you teach these students in such a high-pace and
pressure situation?" The nurse replied, "We use the
method of 'See one, Do one, and Teach one.' We want
the student to see the procedure; then we expect them
to do the procedure as we watch, and then we observe
as they teach the procedure to a new student."

I have found the same technique to be very valuable in coaching prospective leaders. Let's use the
example of taking a new candidate through the process of a presentation. I begin by showing the presentation and explaining the process. After I feel the
person has a good understanding, I will have them
give me the presentation. Once I feel the person is
equipped and ready to do a presentation and before I
send them out to do the presentation, I will bring in
another new staff member and have the person I just
instructed teach the new person. No matter what the
job requirement, this process is proven and ensures
duplication. The candidate being groomed for leadership will "own" the information rather than just
"repeating" the information.

It has been said that more than 90% of those
working to teach leadership will perform steps one
and two, showing and having candidates respond,
but never use step three which is the most significant
part of the process. Any organization that applies the
see it, do it, teach it method will find personal per-

formance taking a quantum leap. The question I am always asking: "Have I personally ensured that everyone I have given leadership instruction has not only witnessed the teaching and performed the teaching but also taught the procedure or skill?" It's amazing how the performance level increases just by adhering to this simple method.

Teaching vs. Coaching

As leaders we must be very careful to understand the difference between teaching and coaching. A teacher is one who presents the material with little or no response from those they are teaching. Many schools today are teaching only to prepare students to pass a standardized test—they teach the test. This forces the students to simply memorize rather than internalize information.

The difference between teaching and coaching is the assurance that the student not only understands the information being taught but has the ability to take the information and impart it to others. Many in leadership positions believe the longer they keep the students in class, the better they will absorb the data. However, the length of the delivery has no relationship to the quality of the content.

On more than one occasion, an organization has asked me to speak by requesting "We need you to fill an hour." I usually chuckle and respond, "Fine, I will do the same talk three times." Unless I am presenting a seminar, it is my belief I should never hold an audience in one position for more than thirty minutes.

Even when I am presenting seminars, I provide frequent breaks. I guarantee that if any "Generation Y" members are in the audience, I better have my "stuff" together; they will move quickly to text messaging if I do not get their attention in the first twenty seconds.

Tower Power

During my football days we met every morning and afternoon at the practice field to go over various techniques and drills. We called these two-a-days.

The specialty coaches were on the field working with the players, while up on the sixty-foot tower stood the head coach. He observed each player and made notes, and at the same time he watched his coaches as they carried out his game plan. We would often hear him shout words of encouragement to his coaches.

So it is with a good CEO or leader. He or she should not only be observing the employees and those under the authority of their leadership but also encouraging the leadership team that has the responsibility of carrying out the marketing plan or strategy. Business today is a moving target—marketing plans and employees are being corrected while the plan is being built. Gone are the days of writing a business plan or marketing plan and giving it a year to see if it will materialize. From the time a new strategy is created and execution begins, the obsolescence clock starts ticking. The timing for the release of a new idea or product is as critical as the product itself.

As a business strategist, I believe the majority of corporate or organizational challenges can be solved by the existing leadership team if they have been properly trained and if there is someone at the table who has "tower power," a leader who has the ability to hear and see things management might overlook, a leader who can offer a fresh look at existing challenges. Here's a step-by-step process for making that happen:

* *Create.* Sometimes a leader lacks the passion to make a project work—he or she creates the idea and passes it off to a subordinate. I often say, "When you remove the creator from the creation, the creation will die." The creator of the project, the one who gave birth to the idea, must stay involved if the project is to have life and succeed. And those who have been selected to execute the project must have equal passion to keep the momentum needed to achieve maximum results. The difference between an idea and a great idea that works is passion. John Wesley summed it up when he said, "Catch on fire with enthusiasm, and people will come for miles to watch you burn." Are you passionate about your project?

* *Evaluate.* Take time to listen to everyone around you; seek the input of those who will be affected by your strategy. Have all the players who can add value to the strategy sit down in the boardroom together, especially those who will be called on to execute the strategy. Companies and organizations often fail to bring new ideas to life because they build their model from the top down instead of from the

bottom up. As you evaluate, you must exercise discernment, perceiving what others overlook. You are the one who has the mental ability to identify and choose what is of value. The time you spend evaluating with your team should be very exciting, creating synergy among those who will be "carrying out the game plan."

* *Formulate.* After you receive all the input from the team, you begin the process of formulating a strategy. The who, what, when, and how. Ask yourself "Who can add value to the strategy? Who can add value by endorsing the project? Who might desire to sponsor the project? What is the purpose of the new strategy, defined in fewer than ten words? What measurements and performance standards must be set to ensure progress? How will I mentor those who will execute the plan?"

* *Initiate.* Recently I happened to catch a short segment of Jeff Foxworthy's TV show. On the show was Larry the Cable Guy, who continually uses the statement "Git-R-Done." Amazing as it may sound, this is where most organizations collapse in the process—the "execution." You can spend weeks or months creating and evaluating and formulating the finest strategy conceived and still fail. If you expect your plan to work, you must have a leadership team in place. They must understand the upside and potential downside of the plan. Every week you, the leader, must mentor your team, edify

your team, and continue to encourage their performance. You must listen to their needs as they move the process forward. Execution is impossible if those being called on to carry out the plan are not totally on board. It is our job as the leader to keep the direction and drive in the project.

* *Celebrate.* Once you have properly positioned the new strategy and all seems to be moving in the direction you desire, take time to thank each and every member who contributed. Take them to a nice dinner, personally address every individual at the table, and tell each person how valuable they were to the process. You have heard it said, "People don't care how much you know until you show them how much you care." I look at the end of each project as the beginning of building a team for the next project. When you recognize and reward those who helped you achieve a goal, you get a higher level of commitment for future projects.

The leader of an organization is the one who has the "tower power," the vantage point from which to oversee both the project and the people; however, outstanding coaches will at times come down from the "tower" to encourage the players and assistant coaches and offer a personal pat on the back to those on the field.

Technique that Duplicates Leaders

One of my more enjoyable and successful business ventures was establishing a company that went around the United States filming "specialty football coaches" from major universities. I would go to such schools as Notre Dame, Nebraska, Oklahoma, UCLA, and others to record a one-hour video with each specialty coach. For example, I produced videos featuring the defensive ends coach at Notre Dame, the defensive middle guard coach from Nebraska, the receivers coach from Louisiana State University. I sat down with each coach to interview him on his techniques and discuss in detail what drills he would perform with his young talent.

It was amazing to see the difference in personalities; some were loud in voicing their direction while others were soft in their instruction. What I did find in every coach was a common golden thread: no matter their style, each would not only coach the young man in the drill, but they would actually perform the desired task. They ensured that each young person had a strong working knowledge of the technique needed to become proficient at their task.

Another great example of teaching technique by modeling was when I was working on my pilot's license. First we established a goal of the number of hours needed to fly solo in the airplane. Each day I would show up at the airport and meet my mentor. He would walk with me around the airplane showing what to check for the preflight. He never left anything to chance. Each and every time he would walk around the airplane with me until he knew beyond all doubt that I was knowledgeable in what to examine for the preflight.

He would continue to do the same once in the plane. He sat in the right seat and put me in the left seat, having me repeat back to him each time I touched a dial or scanned the instruments telling him what I was doing. I remember the day when I experienced my first "power on" stall, a drill where the pilot applies full power to the airplane while pulling back on the yoke causing the nose of the aircraft to go straight into the sky above. The plane suddenly stalls and starts falling like a rock toward the ground. (Needless to say, this is a drill to practice before lunch.)

As I moved on and received my instrument and multiengine ratings, the techniques became more challenging but the teaching remained constant. Never was I given responsibility for personal performance until my mentor (flight instructor) was assured I could perform the requirements necessary to fly the plane with high proficiency.

After consulting for numerous companies, it has become more apparent why some companies have a seemingly perfect execution while others continually struggle to engage their plans. Unlike sports, life, and flying, we leave all the teaching of techniques to boardrooms. Seldom do we find those in leadership taking those they mentor into the field and giving what we would call "real world" instruction. There is no way on God's green earth that someone could understand a "full throttle stall" in a boardroom or classroom, and it is equally impossible for that person we mentor to become proficient in a "real world" sales technique or accounting procedure without "real life" training. We are allowing our high tech video world to substitute for one-on-one coaching of techniques.

Our boardrooms and conference rooms are filled with creative "paper" ideas, business plans, and marketing proposals. And they are often presented by someone in leadership who has never been on the field. I once heard a CEO who fit this description remark that "We must stop training and begin coaching." My response was, "It is impossible to be a good coach unless you have been a player." We cannot implement our paper ideas and expect positive results without first putting them to the real test of personal execution.

Those who "live it" will become greater coaches than those who only "teach it." This leads me to ask, "If you were going into an 'air battle' tomorrow, would you rather be coached by a person who has been there and performed the techniques required or by a person who has zero hours in the cockpit?" We must ensure throughout our organization that our leaders not only coach but also lead by example, demonstrating the proper technique and the expected results. Too often we leave potential success to chance. We cannot duplicate leaders by leaving techniques to chance.

Duplication Requires Dreams

As we move forward in the process of duplicating leaders, it is critically important that we have clear objectives. Breaking down the process and explaining the expectations creates purpose and focus.

Observe successful entrepreneurs and it becomes clear that everything they created began with a dream. I do a monthly audio newsletter where I sign off with the words *dare to dream*. The dream is the beginning of any process. If you are currently successful, reflect back to the beginning of your pilgrimage and you will see that what kept you going when others quit was the dream. The dream is that special place in the mind that we return to when we need to recapture the creative mood necessary to continue when our efforts seem futile. The dream keeps the creative juices flowing. The dream is the *why*, and when the dream is lost we move into the area of doubt and we lose the joy of producing.

Leaders cannot have doubt in their DNA. They must believe in their dreams and look for the vehicle through which to fulfill those dreams. Our life follows our vision, so if our vision is short and futile, our actions have no choice but to follow. What is your dream? What is going to keep you alive when everything around you signals failure? What is going to keep you in the creative state of mind rather than the day-to-day mind of survival? What is going to keep you above the naysayers and doomsayers who continually say you can't do it? A fellow Oklahoman, Garth Brooks, was once asked the question, "How do you handle critics?" His response has been ingrained in my mind: "I never listen to those who have put their dreams on a closet shelf only to have them collect dust over their lifetime."

In the late 1900s, boll weevils destroyed all the cotton in Alabama. The pesky insects destroyed everything related to growing cotton. After sitting around and feeling miserable about what happened, one of the farmers began to ask, "What if we grew something the boll weevil would not eat?" After a few short months they determined peanuts would be the perfect crop, and soon they began to make more money in a shorter period of time than when they were planting cotton.

As you move toward your dream, there will be those who say you can never achieve it or that you are insane for thinking the way you do. But I want you to look at those detractors and see them as pesky little boll weevils that you will overcome as you make your dreams come true. It costs no money to dream, so dream big and you will see your plans come to life.

Duplication Requires Plans

Out of our dreams we create our plans, or what I call the day-to-day activity that must be implemented to fulfill our dreams. Like an architect, we must set up a daily, weekly, and monthly calendar of what must be accomplished in order to make our dreams reality. What separates the leader from the follower is what I call the "grunt work," the daily drills that make us better leaders and show the example required to keep our leadership team inspired.

As we turn on our big screen televisions and watch Phil Mickelson on Sunday, he looks great, walks with confidence, and has that special smile on his face as pressure builds. What we do not see are the hours of hitting balls, examining practice video, and sitting just to study the landscape of the next golf course he is to play, the hours spent thinking through the process of which club is best at what distance, the times Band-Aids were needed to stop the bleeding of his fingers after hitting thousands of practice balls at the driving range.

I am sure Phil has a dream, and you can rest assured he has defined specific objectives for each day as he works his plan to remain the best golfer in the world. Show me a successful athlete, teacher, actor, or anyone who has risen to a degree of success, and I will show you hours spent planning.

A leader's plans will change many times during a month, but the dream will remain constant. At the beginning of each month, take a monthly calendar and establish detailed plans for that month.

What are the hours I wish to target for this project?

Who are the people I need for this project?

Where are the supporting tools I will need to accomplish this project?

What must be reorganized in my calendar to complete this project?

What are the financial resources required to complete the project?

What is the target date I wish to have the project completed?

An example: When I am writing, I know that I must dedicate three hours a day to writing and two hours a day for additional research for the book. I know I must create a place free from distraction and phones, and I plan on writing 2000–3000 words per day. I understand I will need a great laptop, and I determine in advance the financial commitment required to get the proper public relations in place to promote the book. My plan is to have the final manuscript in the hands of my publisher by the end of next month. This is my process of defining specific actions that will accomplish my plan in order to fulfill my dream.

At the end of each month reevaluate your plans, and if needed, reestablish them for the next month. We often do not accomplish all of our plans, but remember, for the leader it is about recovery, not defeat. We make adjustments and move forward. Leaders must continue this process until they reach their dreams and should actively mentor this process to those they are grooming as next-generation leaders.

What can leaders learn from the original plan of duplication?

"Jesus recruited twelve, one quit, and the organization continues to grow today."

Christianity continues to expand today as a result of the original eleven men who were recruited and stayed on message because the message was *simple, sincere, and secure.*

Simple. We complicate our lives today. As one business associate shared, "Once I got out of the way, my business exploded." We tend to study things to death; we spend hours creating a plan for execution and we remain in the planning process for such a long period of time our competitor moves forward. Lee Iacocca once commented, "The timing for the release of a product can be far more important than the development of the product itself." We can also rob our ideas of simplicity by changing the ideas or marketing plan excessively. I am a firm believer that the performance of all projects, marketing concepts, and business plans must be evaluated often. However, if an organization makes multiple changes over a short period of time, it tends to place leaders within the organization in a difficult position. Remember, leaders must not only understand the change but then must execute the change in the organization.

Depending on the size of the organization, we often see one concept being totally accepted only to find another change behind it. Leaders who make change after change establish "analysis/paralysis" in their corporation or organization.

Frequent change can send a signal that those at the top have little understanding of what it takes to make the organization engage. So it behooves the leader to keep the message and methodology extremely simple.

Sincere. The message of the eleven was sincere, from their hearts, not only from their heads. High sales of personal performance books reveal that people are looking for a sincere message on how to improve their lives. The success of *The Purpose Driven Life* is a great example of how millions of people are looking for something that offers real answers, and the book stands the test of "reason." Believing that repetition is the mother of all skills, I shall repeat: People are not impressed with how much you know until they know how much you care. We have all stood in the presence of a person in a position of leadership who shares a message from his head instead of his heart. He or she is more concerned with how they sound and how they look than how they can help those receiving the message. The original eleven were intensely sincere.

Secure. The message was about security. One of the strongest traits of a good leader is making sure that their followers feel secure with the direction of the plans. The fear of loss is always greater than the desire for gain; people want a message that the plans they are pursuing will produce personal security. Can you honestly state that the corporate message you are delivering confirms that you are doing all you can to offer security to those under your mentorship? Do you have support systems in place to assist your people? Can they come to you and share what they think about the direction of the organization—without having fear that what they say would exclude them from any future dialog with you or others in leadership?

As leaders we need to covet people in our organization who present views that are different from ours; we can be certain that the existing competition has a different view and is working day and night to determine how to implement that view. Wouldn't it be a shame if the viewpoint being offered by an existing employee or leader within your organization was the exact plan your competitor was creating to strike a blow to your growth and success? Because many of today's leaders believe they hold "all truth," they continue to lose their best and their brightest to organizations and corporations that listen to their employee's ideas and capitalize on them. Does your message offer security to those under your mentorship?

So let us learn from an organization created more than 2000 years ago and follow that "original plan" for duplicating leaders: keep the execution simple, sincere, and secure.

Leaders Promote on Performance not Favoritism

On the journey to duplicate leadership, it is important to select those to mentor based upon their current personal performance and desire to learn, not on favoritism. Many corporations and organizations make the unforgivable mistake of moving their children into the organization and assigning them a leadership position without getting them well-grounded in the skills necessary to maintain the organization or corporation, and more importantly without earning the respect of the existing leadership team.

If this is your current challenge, always remember that your children will never be accepted until they have proven themselves to those they will lead. If you are the current CEO of an organization and you are grooming your kids, have them perform every given task within the organization. In the past, I happened to be a part of a company that experienced an amazing transition. The founder of the company started his children, right out of college, in the process. He had his children spend four to six months in each department from loading trucks, R&D, information systems, accounting, legal, shipping, and most importantly, since it was a sales organization, his children had to go out and develop successful sales relationships. Setting an example as followers made them easily received as leaders. If this process is not established, it can create multiple divisions within the organization, which will have a negative effect on growth.

Another way many organizations put the skids on growth is by going outside the company, recruiting people, and giving them advantages the current leadership team does not enjoy. Once again I have seen this first hand—a large company determining that their current leadership team was not fulfilling the requirements necessary to move the company to better bottom-line profits. So the company puts on a major recruiting drive, even paying for people to come in and help "to move the company forward." Here was the backfire: It was done without the knowledge of the existing leadership team, done without first sitting down and determining the problems that were causing slow sales, and it was performed in a way that sent a loud message to the existing team, "You no longer have value." Once again, it was done with a focus on bottom-line profit instead of working with the people who created the profit.

The results were disastrous. First, every one of the people recruited failed and not one remained with the company. So not only did the company lose from the position of trying to replace their current leadership, they also broke trust with their existing leadership, which even to this day they have not restored and will never restore until they change their philosophy from "me down" leadership to the "bottom up" creation of leaders.

As you can imagine, many of the leaders that were once in their organization have now moved on to a competitor and have become quite successful. Like my old football coach who had all the talent in the locker-room but could never win, they did not understand how to coach those who were under their guidance.

Dictators Centralize Power, Leaders Decentralize

"Me down" leadership, or what is often referred as command and control, was created hundreds of years ago; it was called "Centralization of Power." When you look at the communist countries you find this method of leadership. It concentrates all the power of an organization in one person or a small group of people and imposes rules and regulations that are not favorable to those responsible for enforcing the rules. This kind of power is often found in organizations where the leader has never personally performed the task he is asking of the people. The result is compulsory rules that actually deplete the enthusiasm and passion of those who are requested to perform the task.

The "I am" personality and the "I have" personality combine to become "I am the leader and I have all the answers." One would think this archaic style of leadership would be gone in the 21st century, but surprisingly it is still alive. Those using this style of leadership have a very high pride level, an underlying arrogance rather than confidence precedes their actions. But as it is said, "Pride goes before the fall of a man." I say it more simply: "Never allow your ego to replace your common sense."

The organizations and corporations that show the strongest degree of success and have created an atmosphere for duplicating leadership have been those that *decentralize* power. They seek to learn from listening more than speaking. For the most part they employ the code of "quick to listen, slow to speak, and slow to anger." They are the leaders who work to create relationships on a deeper level, as in the stories of Bill Marriott Jr. and Southwest Airlines; they see their success in developing the success of others. They have the attitude that it is better to create stars than to be the star.

Leaders (or what I would rather call people in leadership positions) who subscribe to the centralized method of leadership, will ultimately see failure. If you have no relationships with those who can create results, and if those who can create results are not allowed to offer input, you have lost the key to your success. That key is servanthood.

Duplicating the leadership team must begin with the head of the organization, and it must be a major focus. The mission statement each day should be, "How do I make my people better? What tools or message can I create to add value to each person under my leadership?"

If we're not getting the desired results, we should first ask, "What am I doing wrong with my people, not with my marketing plan or products and service?" True leaders will always examine themselves first before looking at others. Be the type of leader who moves people from the position of faith and hope, not fear.

There are scores of bright people sitting at this very moment in boardrooms and meeting rooms across the world not saying what needs to be said because of fear. The fear is that their statements would put them on a "black list" or devalue them in the next employee evaluation. So out of fear they sit and nod, not giving vital information that could add value to the performance of the organization. Then they leave the room and say to their associates, "Can you believe that ignorant baboon?" They return to their office or to the field of activity with zero passion, excitement, or belief in the direction of the leaders.

What they do know without any doubt is that they are way down the food chain when it comes to importance to the organization. They will now take the energy they once gave to the organization and begin looking for other options for income. I have no argument with creating accountability within an organization, and often that requires rules and regulations, but we should never create these rules and regulations with the intent to hurt those who are employed as our leadership. The question I have for those who are in positions of leadership and have chosen to operate in this manner is one asked daily around the office by those you are leading: "Why should I be led by you?"

The Four R's of Duplication

Growing up we heard that we must go to school and learn the three R's: Reading, Writing, and Arithmetic. It has always interested me that two of the three don't begin with R. (They just share that strong R phoneme.) I want to ask you to consider another set of R's—four R's that actually begin with R.

Reason-Research-Record-Relate

No matter who is in my audience, I make sure that I share the four R's. I have found that in today's climate they have been neglected, and yet they are essential in the development and duplication of leaders.

Reason. "Come let us reason together." If I have seen a decline in any one skill, it would be the ability to reason. Let's face it, reasoning skills are not taught in schools. They might be found to a small degree in a math class, but the bridge between math and the reality of day-to-day life is difficult. Understanding how to find the square root of two does not help one determine how to make payroll on Monday when the cash is short.

I found a rather simple example of this when my wife and I were at a restaurant. While we waited to be seated, the manager asked the couple in front of us if they desired a "booth or table." It was amazing to see their hesitancy as they worked through the mental processes to determine where to sit. I was thankful they weren't deciding for an entire group.

As we watch the US Congress and Senate add "pork" to seemingly good bills we ask, "What is the reasoning behind this decision?" When we see people purchase homes beyond their income we ask, "Where is the reasoning behind this?" When loan officers lend money knowing the consumers do not have the ability to repay, we ask, "Where is the reasoning behind this?" We recently saw on the news that border patrol agents were sentenced to prison for ten years for shooting an illegal drug dealer. "Where is the reasoning behind this?" We look at Wall Street where men and women with outstanding financial intellect abuse their power and destroy the lives of thousands, and again, "Where is the reasoning behind this?"

Each day, as leaders, we must make decisions based on our reasoning skills. When I am teaching, I always begin by asking people to question what I am teaching them. "Does it make sense? Does what you are hearing line up with your head, heart and gut?"

This is the internal switch that must be in the "on" position each hour of the day. Reasoning must have perfect alignment in the following three faculties: *head, heart, and gut.* Does what I am hearing make sense *mentally*, is it *morally* correct, and does it sit well *physically?*

Research. We have become a rather gullible nation. In many cases, we hear a newsperson state something on air, and we accept it as fact. We sit in our colleges and hear professors make comments based on their personal beliefs, and we accept their opinions as facts. We listen to political candidates and take their promises as facts. As leaders we must always research what we hear before making decisions. A good example can be found in the emails we receive each day.

I remember on one occasion someone sent me an email about a potential presidential candidate. The message contained something quite alarming. "Send this to as many people as possible," it read. Fortunately, I made a couple of phone calls and found out the allegation was unfounded. I wondered how many people passed on the message without researching the facts.

As you climb the corporate ladder there will be times when you will hear or read negative comments about a fellow employee or associate. Never pass judgment or continue the negative conversation; get the facts before commenting on any situation. With the Internet and the many other avenues of communication available, it is easy to research information that is driven by "hearsay."

We must train our people to research and make the ability to research a requirement for any person in a position of leadership.

Record. I enjoy speaking to groups in Japan. From the beginning of my talk to the end, my audiences there continually take notes and record my every word. It is somewhat humorous since the translation will often delay the message to the crowd, and so when I tell a joke I see them writing down every word. But recording is what I consider to be a key in the development of a leader, and when I speak of recording, I mean physically writing down what you hear.

In today's high-tech society, we have lost this art and so have lost the ability to own information. When a leader reads or hears a message containing something that could help him or her, it is to their advantage to record it. I am never without my yellow pad as I drive down the road and listen to leadership material on a CD or in a radio program related to leadership. I also keep a yellow marker close to my side when I am reading a book or an article so that I can immediately highlight a point of interest and later record it on my yellow pad. One might ask, "What is the big deal? Why would you want to record something that is already in print?" I have found that taking ownership of the material I read by moving it from my mind onto paper helps me internalize it at a much greater rate.

Relate. After applying reasoning to information, researching information, and recording information, you can begin to extract what you wish to use and what you desire to communicate to others. Thousands of outstanding men and women have a great depth of knowledge, but they fall short in their ability to relate that information to others.

I had just returned from military service when I decided to return to college. After being absent from the academic environment for years, it was important that I choose classes that would be meaningful but not stressful to ease my transition. Looking through the directory I read the words Speech 101, a beginning speech course. I enrolled and it turned out to be a course I will remember for the rest of my life.

It was one of those classes that held around 300 students, and we sat in assigned seats so they could check our attendance. On the first day of class, as the throng of students waited for the professor to arrive, we casually chatted about life on campus. Suddenly, a voice resonated from the back of the auditorium; a man was walking between the seats, moving toward the front of the classroom and welcoming our presence.

As the semester progressed, I became more than just a student to the professor as he recognized that I was older than the other students and had just returned from the service. One day after class, he asked me why I appeared to be so bored. I explained to him that having just returned from the service and being some-what older than my freshman class, I just didn't have the excitement they had. Most of them were excited because they were finally away from home more than because they were going to college, and I had lost that thrill the first night in my military bunk. He said, "Let's take a walk."

We went to the top of the four-story mathematics and engineering building next door, and we talked as we walked up and down each hallway. As we walked he shared his philosophy with me. When we reached the first floor, he said, "Bob, in this building are the finest minds on campus; the average IQ would astound you. Many of these students will be hired by major corporations immediately upon graduation. Great minds, great opportunities, but for the most part they will never have the communication skills they need to make rapid advancement or to become entrepreneurs. Bob, those who master the ability to communicate will always be on top; they will always be in demand, and will always be in control of their destiny."

I determined from that day forward to become a great communicator and to always have the ability to take the information I learned and relate it to others. Anyone who wishes to become a great leader must learn how to relate to others and learn the skill of communication.

As leaders, especially those who are working to duplicate new leaders, we must use the filter of the four R's. These will act as our grid for personal performance so we can continually check ourselves and our new leaders.

Staying with the Basics
Remaining in the Creative State of Mind

Golf is about keeping your head down; basketball, keeping yourself between the goal and the person you're guarding; football is about "breaking down," and college wrestling is about finding your base; flying is about "fly the plane first," and wellness is about eating "lean and green."

As leaders, we will continually seek new adventures and exciting opportunities, and we must train those leaders we mentor to do the same. That 2 a.m. wake-up call, not the one from our alarm clock but the one from our mental clock when the next thought or idea strikes, should never cease if we are leaders. But as we continue to move forward and experiment with new concepts and ideas, we still must remember the basics for building leaders. We have the responsibility to keep our organization or corporation secure by practicing the basics that ensure stability. We are the master teacher, the one who has been chosen to assist others to become the best they can be. Our job is to ensure that core values and sound reasoning are taught to each new generation in our organizations.

Followers Hope to Win; Leaders Expect to Win

Jack Welch, the CEO's CEO, is famous for his business acumen and straight-from-the-gut management style. Among his many pearls of wisdom are the five keys to success: One, control your destiny or someone else will. Two, face reality as it is, not as it was or as you wish it to be. Three, be candid with everyone. Four, don't manage, lead. And five, change before you have to.

On an overseas flight I found myself thinking about why some people make it in life and others never achieve the degree of success that is possible. As I sat in the first class section of the Singapore 747–400 and looked about the cabin, I counted 22 people. The rest of the plane held more than 300 people. What mental decision separated the 22 from the others? Sure, I realized that some in first class were gifted the seat by their corporation, and I was confident that some in

THE POWER OF LAYERED LEADERSHIP

the back of plane could be in the front, but as in life, why do only a few succeed?

I often pose this question to my audiences and have received hundreds of varied answers. Is success determined by fate, luck, genetics, ability, or some combination of the four? As I flew that night, I reflected on my past and thought of the many successful people I have known. By the time the plane landed I had settled on what I believed to be the major attribute successful people have and others do not.

When I arrived at my international venue I wanted to test my theory, so I began my speech by asking members of the audience to raise their hands if they hoped to win in business and life. Everyone in the room lifted their hands. Then I said, "If you hope to win, chances are very slim that you'll ever see success." There was a murmuring among the audience as attendees looked at each other, wondering whether or not the interpreter had accurately translated my words.

I went on to explain that the majority of unsuccessful businesses and organizations as well as unsuccessful relationships failed because those involved *hoped* for success. When you use the word "hope," your mind automatically sets up an escape route. The mind recognizes that success is not definite and that failure is a possibility. This quickly translates into, "Failing is okay because it's an acknowledged possibility." Is it any wonder that failure usually ensues?

In my many conversations around the world it is obvious that people are setting themselves up for failure by using the word "hope." "I hope this marriage works." "I hope I can stop drinking alcohol." "I hope I can make it through school." "I hope my new business concept is accepted." I feel safe in saying that winners never enter any arena "hoping." Think of Phil Mickelson or Michael Jordan. Can you hear them saying "Boy, I sure hope I win today"? What do they say?

As William Arthur Ward, the noted American pastor and teacher, once observed, "People never plan to be failures; they simply fail to plan to be successful."

If we change our vocabulary from "hoping" to "expecting," our mind is there to reward us. The brain says, "There is no way out. I have to succeed. I must make this happen." The statement "I expect" prompts the brain to begin setting up a route for success and the endorphins start to flow. Test this concept at this very moment; make a statement using the word "hope" three times. Then make the same statement using the word "expect" three times. Feel your endorphins enlisting that additional energy.

Now take a look at those around you who have failed, and ask yourself whether or not they simply *hoped* to win. I've always maintained that if we get the person right, the business or life will work. It's all about people. We, the people, make the choice to either "hope" to win or "expect" to win. How many times in life have we sabotaged ourselves by using the word "hope"?

I grew up in a 400-square-foot home, and I remember that even as a small child I would look at my surroundings and say, "I expect more." From elementary school forward I have always worked "expecting" to achieve more than those around me. This simple key is that everyone who succeeds comes to a place in their life where they make a conscious choice to "expect" better things instead of "hoping" for things to get better. We as leaders ensure that those we coach begin to speak from the position of expecting instead of hoping.

So, what are the qualities that characterize people who expect to win?

Expectation is engraved in their mindset. They think and operate with expectations, not hope. They become self-governed, or as many would say self-disciplined, in their actions and thoughts. They continually seek information that will add value to them as a person and those they are mentoring. They seek those of like mind who can help expand their thinking processes, from day-to-day life to organizational and performance skills. School is never out for those who expect to win. They do not have the "I must find out all the answers myself and prove to others" attitude; instead they seek synergy from other leaders and people who can add value.

Maintaining this "I expect" attitude is a challenge, just as it has been for those in leadership before us. We all have come from educational systems, families, employment, or perhaps even churches where we have been taught from a position of hope instead of expectation. I foresee that one of the major challenges for the future will be taking hundreds of thousands of outstanding and talented people from the pits of "hoping" to the pleasures of "expecting."

They are personally self-governing. We hear the word "government" today, but when was the last time you heard the term "self-government"? As leaders who continue to build leaders, we need to establish this word in our personal vocabulary. People who expect to win are willing to take personal responsibility and become self-governed persons of integrity. It has been humorous but frankly sad to witness the sitting US Congress and Senate explaining our current problems.

At the time of this writing we are witnessing a complete meltdown of our financial institutions due to individuals in lending organizations failing to apply self-government. Billions of dollars have been loaned to homebuyers by lenders who knew that the chances of these loans being repaid were futile. Thus begins the blame game—lenders are blaming government for making them grant the loans; borrowers are blaming the lenders for not making them aware of certain conditions of the loans; one political party is blaming the other political party, with absolutely no one at the moment stepping up and taking personal responsibility.

Since Adam first shrugged off responsibility by blaming his wife, telling God, "Eve made me do it," self-government and personal responsibility have been in a continual downward spiral. If you expect to win, however, you have to take responsibility—and the first person you have to take responsibility for is you. Look in the mirror and acknowledge that you alone are ultimately responsible for the direction your life takes. Look in the mirror and say, "Before I place blame on

others I will first examine how I function as a leader."
Franklin Roosevelt said, "The buck stops here." Those
in current leadership positions in Washington today
say, "Keep the buck moving so it won't stop here."
Anyone who expects to win as a leader must acknowledge personal responsibility in every decision.

They expect to be rewarded. There are rewards for
expecting to win. One is the reward of believing in
yourself. I was asked during one of my conferences on
leadership, "What about competition?" I responded
by saying, "If you believe in yourself, have a plan for
moving forward, and expect to win, you have no competition." When you expect to win, your self-esteem
is strong and your actions are clear. You know you will
face competition every day, but if you wake up in the
morning knowing the day is yours, your mind will stay
focused on your plan rather than potential conflict.

There will be times when some will not understand the "new you," the person of confidence and
high expectations. Many will confuse your confidence
with arrogance, but remain strong knowing that
you are on the path from mediocrity to excellence.
Remain strong as a leader, enjoying the success you
have gained, and continue helping your future leaders
achieve their personal goals. What greater reward is
there than helping others move up the ladder of leadership with the "I expect" attitude? The challenges
will be many, but the reward will prove greater.

Passion, Purpose, Possibility, and Practice

*"To every man there comes a special moment when he
is figuratively tapped on the shoulder and offered that
chance to do a very special thing, unique to him and
fitted to his talents. What a tragedy if that moment
finds him unprepared or unqualified to do the work
that could have been his finest hour."*

—*Winston Churchill*

One of the greatest obstacles to building a successful
leadership program in any industry is the very human
tendency to say, "Someday I will…" or "In a year or
two, I'm going to…" Unfortunately, someday rarely
arrives because we always have plenty of excuses for
not beginning new enterprises. "I'm too busy right
now" is a comment I have heard more times than I
can actually count, and often it comes from a well-
meaning and talented individual. Our calendar shows
Sunday through Saturday, but I have never found
"Someday" listed.

I call this the "when I feel like it" syndrome. I
have a hired man who helps around my ranch on trac-
tor work. He is quite remarkable given the fact that he
only finished the third grade in school. He has done
quite well, owning all of his equipment and having
clients lined up for his services. I remember calling
him one day in the winter, and I could hear in his
voice that he was suffering from a cold. I immediately
said, "Wow, John, it sounds like you have a severe
cold. I'll call you back for some work when you are
feeling better."

His mindset was crystal clear when in a raspy voice he responded, "What's feelings got to do with it? I will be there within the hour." A third-grade-educated man left a message chiseled in stone on my brain: "What's feelings got to do with it?" If we wait to move toward the next challenge based on feelings, we will never move forward. Success as a leader is always asking the question, "What am I doing that my competitor is not doing in order to be where they will never be?" Building a successful leadership team and organization, whether it is a Fortune 100 company, church, or a main street company, must be done with the passion of saying, "No matter how I feel, I will get up and get moving. I will challenge myself each day. I will work to become a better leader."

The leader of an organization or company must live it, breathe it, and be passionate about it on a daily basis. Great performers, athletes, teachers, and other successful individuals who have been placed in leadership positions demonstrate that *passion overrides how they feel.* They are passionate about what they do. It's the kind of passion that pushes athletes to rise at 4:30 a.m. for practice and inspires teachers to stay up late preparing their lessons for the following day. That kind of passion can actually alter direction or provide the infusion of energy needed to change the entire course of a group or company.

Passion is the first of the Four "P"s that create a winner in any field. Passion is obvious in the way a person sits, walks, and talks. It's that indescribable something that ignites a person from within and shines outward. It shows up in the way a runner concentrates, not on his sore muscles, but solely on the finish line. It is evident in the way a medical researcher focuses not on the disease but the cure.

We all know that it's easy to be positive and gracious when we're winning; it's far more difficult when things aren't going our way. If we pay attention to great leaders we will discover time and again that they maintain their passion and positive attitude and they *keep moving forward.*

So, what is it that motivates leaders to keep moving forward despite setbacks? I call it purpose.

Purpose is the second "P" leaders have in common. They have a clear purpose in mind, one that stays firmly on the horizon despite the swells and troughs of uneven seas. They don't fall back on excuses such as "I can't because of my current situation."

When I hear someone say they would like to be successful but don't have the time due to their "unique" circumstances, I think "Welcome to average." Everyone on this earth can find a reason not to succeed, but for those of us who have been born in North America, there is no excuse. Each of us faces challenges and hardships throughout our life, yet the most successful leaders will not accept obstacles as insurmountable; they will figure out a way to go around them or over them or any way that keeps them moving forward.

Leaders must envision the end goal. They must clearly see the *possibilities*—the third "P." During the rapid pace of each day it can be easy to get distracted by issues that arise and divert our focus from possibilities to problems. As leaders, we can enter a room full of passion and begin discussing the possibility of our proposal, and Bingo! There will be someone in the room who wishes to focus on the negative effect instead of the positive possibility of success. I do believe it is necessary to dissect every proposal, running the process through the earlier mentioned "sifting process." But as leaders we should do this carefully, not destroying the creativity of our team. We must always look at the outer limits, not the limitations, and train our young leaders to do the same.

The final "P" is *practice*. Think of all the times you've watched someone do something well and thought to yourself, "They make it look easy." As a professional speaker, I often interact with people who say, "You make it seem effortless. Your message was so clear and presented with such passion." I cannot speak for the thousands who share platforms across the world, but for each minute I am on the platform I have spent twenty minutes in preparation and practice.

Let me share some outstanding news. You might never be a Michelangelo or Van Gogh, but you no doubt could paint fairly well if you took the time to study under a good teacher and were willing to practice. As with any dream or goal, you have to ask yourself how badly you want it and what you are willing to sacrifice in order to achieve it. Are you willing to let go of excuses and commit to the four "P"s?

In his book *Day by Day with Charles Swindoll,* the well-known theologian and author reflects, on January 1, that "An old year has completed its course. A new year is smiling at us with twelve months of the unknown, an entire ocean of possibilities, including both sun-drenched days and a few storms with howling winds and giant waves stretched out across the uncharted waters. If we let ourselves, we could become so afraid of the potential dangers, so safety-conscious, that we would miss the adventure."

Take hold of your life as a leader, being very careful how you live it, not as an unwise person but wise, making the most of every opportunity. Reach outside your comfort zone, reach for the endless possibilities that wait for you, hold the vision not only for yourself but for those who depend on you.

Deleting Bad Habits
Knowing What *Not* To Do

"*I am your constant companion. I am your greatest helper or I am your heaviest burden. I will push you onward or I will drag you down to failure. I am completely at your command. Half of the things you do, you might just as well hand over to me and I will be able to do them much quicker. I am not easily managed. You must really be firm with me. Show me exactly how you want something done and after a few lessons I will do it automatically. I am the servant of all great men and women and, alas, of all failures as well. Those who are great—I have made great. Those who are failures—I have made failures. I am not a machine, although I*"

111

work with all the precision of a machine plus the intelligence of a man. You can run me for profit or you can run me for ruin, it makes no difference to me. Take me, train me, be firm with me and I will place the world at your feet. Be easy with me and I will destroy you. Who am I? I am habit."

—*Anonymous*

Success comes to those who habitually do things that unsuccessful people never do. Benjamin Disraeli said, "Nurture your mind with great thoughts, for you will never go any higher than you think." Your life today is a result of your thinking yesterday. Your life tomorrow will be determined by what you think today. When you are willing to change your thinking, you can change your feelings. When you change your feelings, you change your actions. *Changing your actions based on good thinking will revolutionize your life.* Knowledge only has value in the hands of someone who has the ability to reason.

Dr. David Schwartz, motivational expert, says in his book *The Magic of Thinking Big,* "Where success is concerned, people are not measured in inches or pounds, by college degrees, or family background; they are measured by the size of their thinking." One of the reasons people don't achieve their dreams is that they desire to change their results without changing their thinking. Leaders who get results must take dominion of their thoughts and habits.

Sam Walton was told, "You're crazy! In a town with less than 50,000 people? There's no way on God's green earth that this store you're creating will ever last. No way!" Now with stores that employ more than one million people and annual sales in excess of $200 billion, it is obvious that Sam Walton's thinking was far ahead of those around him. Are you allowing your thinking to stoop to the level of those around you?

Albert Einstein said, "The problems that exist in the world today cannot be solved by the level of thinking that created them." Our minds have to continually be thinking of solutions. People with mediocre mindsets think only about survival or maintenance, while successful people are thinking about developing projects that will help other people.

I have heard it said that 97% of all people are non-thinkers. They wake up every morning wondering how to survive while waiting for instructions on how to resume living. Leaders do not have this mindset. They get up each morning looking forward to the challenges and focusing on solutions.

As I boarded a recent flight from Singapore to Los Angles, I sank into a first class seat of the magnificent 747–400. I had finished a very difficult week sharing leadership principles from the platform and was hoping that no one would be seated next to me so I could put my mind in neutral and catch up on some reading. Just before the door closed, a happy gentleman sat down beside me all smiles and ready to talk for the next twelve hours. At first I looked at my personal needs and then thought, "I teach that you learn by listening, and here I am shutting down." So off we went with our conversation. There wasn't any ground we didn't cover: our kids, grandkids, world economy, the

Academy Awards, religion, and facts and fiction about global warming. Before you knew it we were landing in L.A. It wasn't until our landing that we actually introduced ourselves. When I shared my name and extended my hand I asked, "What is your profession?" He said he was a brain surgeon and asked, "What do you do?" I responded by saying, "I am also a brain surgeon; I am a Doctor of Solutions. I assist organizations and corporations on thinking correctly."

As leaders we need to think of ourselves as *Doctors of Solutions,* always ready to offer a remedy for the maladies that hinder our progress or the progress of our companies. I believe some of those hindrances are the *bad habits* we often find in companies and their leaders. And what are some of those bad habits?

Putting a Lid on Leaders

Companies often develop bad habits. One of the worst is not allowing the leaders to offer their personal ideas for the improvement of the organization. We will often see this when an organization or corporation changes a business or marketing plan without allowing input from those it will affect. This type of leadership is typical today; so many restrictions and controls are in place that the leadership team doesn't have the flexibility to support the directives being forced on them.

If this form of delivery continues, a definite division will occur between those sending the message and those receiving the message. If you are this type of executive, you will have their minds but never their respect, and your words will become void and value-less. Once you put a lid on your leaders by barring them from the creative process, you have destroyed the essential tool required to move any strategy for-ward—*your leaders.*

They will come to work or attend your meetings; you will see their bodies, but you will never have their willingness to support your ideas. This is not leader-ship; this is dictatorship from the old archaic school of driving people versus leading people. Your organiza-tion or corporation will ultimately collapse, and sadly many will blame the collapse on their people's poor performance, never seeing that their personal perfor-mance was the true reason for failure.

Hopefully, some will read this and reverse the pro-cess before it is too late. If you have been placing lids on your leaders, you have likely created an environ-ment where your leadership team spends more time putting out flames than creating the fire that could move your organization forward. It is very simple: Either learn how to use your leadership team, or get ready to see them become your competitors.

Changing When the Wind Blows

I have found it amazing to watch organizations and corporations slow down and actually stop growing because they continually change business plans. A financial firm that retained me several years ago had a founder who would make changes constantly. I told him after a couple of months that he was the only person I knew who, if taking a test, would change the questions and the answers before he finished. He could never allow any change to last more than a year or two before he would come up with another idea.

Now hear me, I am all about change. I believe the saying, "It is hard to live with change but impossible to live without it." However, too much change too often can create zero growth. Here is a simple truth: Change takes time and must be tested. If you issue a change in a large organization, it can take twelve to eighteen months to get the change enacted through the entire system. Remember, the change must not only be explained but must be understood in order for it to be effective. In addition, when you make a change, get the blessing of your leadership team who must execute the new strategy. If you move without their acceptance, the change will never occur, and there will be resistance. As leaders, we must take time to allow synergy to produce the energy to implement the change.

Second, if you are a leader who is continually putting new changes in place before the previous changes are working or being effective, you will lose the ability to lead. Sure, you may have a title or you might even own the company, but you will soon find yourself in the position of the fellow who said, "I'm their leader. Which way did they go?" The reason: None of your changes in the past were effective, so how can you expect those you are leading to respect the next change?

Such a basic truth, but so overlooked in today's organizations. Remember, the only effective change comes when those you ask to execute the change are on board and willing to implement the change with passion. If they do not believe in the change, they will go through the motions of implementation but without the "passion that creates the action."

Changes that affect the income of the producers in your organization are the most sensitive. A leader's first question should be, "Is the change I am making good for those who have proven their loyalty and ability to produce, or is the change focused on numbers created on paper?"

The greatest number of emails I receive from corporations around the world relate to changes that directly affect the income of employees in the field. Extreme caution must be exercised when a new company policy or change affects the incomes of those who produce the company's income, especially if the change is perceived to be negative or one made without the involvement of those it affects.

We have all heard of the mid-life crisis; well there seems to be a leadership crisis as those in charge of seemingly successful companies commit financial suicide by initiating programs and policies that put egos ahead of common sense. It seems no one is immune, even those who came up the hard way, in making a successful business appear to have dementia when it comes to monetary adjustments related to their people. There is a saying in sales: "Once you become good at making a profit for your company, the company rewards you by doubling your quota and narrowing your territory." So it is in corporate America, where you will find a company doing quite well, moving along at a good rate of growth, when all of a sudden the founders, CEO, CFO, or board of directors get the idea that the people are making too much money for the amount of work they are doing. Once this thought takes root, you can normally count on a two- to three-year shelf life for the existence of that company.

I will never forget my early days out of college. I went to work for a small company in the town where I attended college. It was a small company, doing perhaps $200,000 to $300,000 in sales. I found a method to increase the sales to $500,000 dollars per year. I went on the road for three years, traveling each week, leaving my wife and child on Sunday night and returning on Friday evening. Then Bingo! The owner pulled me aside, explained that I should be doing more, and presented me with what I call a "paper plan." A paper plan is a plan that looks great on paper, but in reality or the real world it will not survive.

What had happened over the years was what I have found to be true in many organizations: the more successful the organization or corporation becomes the further away from reality the founder or CEO moves. They either have forgotten what it takes to build a strong sales and marketing force and leadership team, or they never did what they expect others to do. They were simply lucky enough early in their career to locate the people who knew how to get the job done. A good sign that the leader at the top is on the wrong path is to see how many leaders within the organization are no longer around.

My former employer, who ran me all over the country, was one of the casualties in this area, for eventually I left the company, created my own company, and took over market dominance in his area while he was still working out his next paper plan. As a leader of an organization, founder, CEO, or board of directors, be careful when you are "messing with" the money of those who created your success. Making an incorrect move will cost you dearly as it has for thousands of corporations before you.

Being "Jack of All Trades"

We as leaders can often fall into the trap of believing we are good in every aspect of the operation of our organization. We have convinced ourselves that without us the marketing plan will fail, without our knowledge the business plan will fail, without us the whole darn place will fall apart. Here is a simple fact I have discovered about myself: I am excellent at two, maybe three, things. I am above average in other things, average in most things, and really stink at some things." As a leader I had to learn that for me to progress and become successful, I needed to surround myself with others who were excellent in the areas that I was not.

We can easily trick ourselves into believing we are the master of all things. If you are the leader of a company that is experiencing slow growth or no growth you may need to reassess your strengths and weaknesses. If you know your product inside and out, and if you can inspire others to believe in your product and promote it, make sales your number one priority. If on the other hand you also believe that you are great when it comes to marketing ideas or concepts, but those around you are not motivated by your message, guess what? It does not take a degree in nuclear science to understand where you perform best. I was contacted by a fellow speaker a couple of years ago who called to say he was asked to speak at a meeting for engineers, and since he was already booked, would I like to speak for their upcoming meeting? I said sure and proceeded to contact the folks who requested a speaker. I spent a couple of hours going over their needs and some of their concerns. I worked day and night trying to come up with something that would give them value, but I just could not make my brain connect with the need.

Against my internal feelings, I went to the event, and in my eyes, it was a complete flop. Now, I am an outstanding speaker on leadership skills, performance skills, and marketing, but addressing the needs of engineers? No way. (My wife and son were at the event and said great things about my delivery, but my wonderful wife finds good things in me no matter what the situation.) If you want your organization to succeed and you are the founder, CEO, or in the top tier of management, do not let your ego get ahead of your common sense and reasoning. Determine quickly where not to work, and surround yourself just as quickly with those who can *excel where you fail.*

Getting Derailed by Details

Never major on the minors. Have you ever found yourself getting up early in the morning with your agenda ready to go only to be derailed by a minor interruption that takes your time away from the bigger issues? If you are reading this book and you have what is referred to as a type "A" personality, you probably believe you must be involved in every action and detail of your business in order to keep the "big wheel rolling." You find yourself doing things and making decisions that should have been delegated to others. As a leader, you must continually keep your mind focused on the major idea at hand.

Everything begins with an idea. Leaders understand that we are constantly in the battle of the mind. We clarify our thoughts and look for the fastest and most secure route to reach our overall plan. We establish our route for the best results, define the timeline, and begin to move forward. We don't allow our great ideas and plans to become derailed while we examine minutiae. I could spend the rest of my life examining the grammar of this book, the spelling, the page layout, and the many other details. However, my job is to supply the content and to set a timeline for the completion of the book, and I cannot afford to major on details that can be handled by those who are trained in other areas. Leaders must be vigilant not to chase the *urgent* at the expense of the *important*. During times of turmoil, leaders must be cautious not to be moved by emotions but governed by the principles that keep them anchored.

On my website, www.BobGoshen.com, you will find a 21-day program for developing new habits. Those who study personal performance have determined that a bad habit can be turned around if one stays consistent for twenty-one days. Using this wisdom, I have created a simple program where you sign up at no cost and each and every day I will come to you via your computer while you sleep. The first thing each morning you will watch a message from me, coaching you on ways to turn bad habits into good ones.

Leaders Find True North When All Seems to be Heading South

Over the public address system I hear, "Ladies and gentlemen, we are on final approach for Moscow Domodedovo Airport. Please fasten seatbelts and turn off all electronic devices." It is a cold day in Moscow, twenty-eight degrees Fahrenheit, snowing, and very cloudy. The current Russian economy is in turmoil. During the past decade Russia has been extremely prosperous with oil prices securing their expenditures and the appetites of the new entrepreneurs. Capitalism exploded beyond anyone's expectation, but now as the world economy has turned south it has created a spirit of fear in the Russian business community. I have come to Russia to share a message with business leaders on what to do when times become challenging. It is a message with universal relevance.

Leaders will experience times when all will not go as planned, and the project or business that began on a positive note will become a major challenge. What does a leader do during these times? I have found five principles that have never changed and, if applied, will keep you focused when times seem a little cloudy.

Basics. After being retained as the new head coach for the Green Bay Packers, Vince Lombardi found himself at his first press briefing. "Mr. Lombardi, what are you going to do to turn this team around? Are you going to let players go? Are you going to change plays? Are you going to rework the management? What are you going to do to make this team a winner?"

In response, Lombardi said, "Gentlemen, I am not going to eliminate any players, I will not change the plays, nor will I insist on management changes. What we will do is throw the football better than anyone in the NFL; we will catch the football better than anyone in the NFL; we will block better and we will tackle better than anyone in the NFL. We will restore the attitude of winning by becoming *brilliant on the basics.*"

When times become challenging it is easy to depart from the basics. For leaders, "the basics" means staying in a creative state of mind, the position that supplies energy to the organization, where we build on how to become better, where we ensure our people become better, where we create strategies of growth and advancement. Often we find leaders who retreat to a survival mentality, focusing on how to protect the bottom-line profits and how to release staff. They fall into the management mind-set instead of the creative mindset. It is essential for leaders to be *brilliant with the basics,* the creative state of mind, and not get wrapped up in the management side of business.

Control. As a leader you need to quickly define the areas you can control and the areas over which you have no control. I had a father who was an alcoholic.

I had the misfortune of seeing firsthand how alcohol can overcome the power of a person. I spent hours trying to rationalize with my father. I begged him, emotionally wept for his departure from the disease, all in vain. I would go to bed thinking about it; I would get up in the morning thinking about it and soon came to the realization I had no control over the situation. No matter what I did, it would ultimately have to be his decision to stop drinking.

Looking back on those years, I now see how they stripped me of creativity. Sadly, we find some in leadership today who focus on areas they can't control. Much of the lack of productivity in business is the direct result of employees who come to work each day mentally focused on areas they have no control over. They spend their time talking about political activity they dislike and how it is creating havoc in their lives, and they waste innumerable hours worrying about events they cannot influence.

As leaders we must recognize *efficiency is related to emotions,* and when our emotions are attached to activities we cannot control, we quickly deplete the energy and creative mind-set required to lead others. I am not saying you should ignore every urgent need, but recognize that the most you might be able to offer is a quick phone call, email, or note, and then move on to help people who welcome your counsel and advice. Over the years, I have found three areas I can positively control that have a direct outcome on my success.

- *Attitude.* Each day I have a choice when I wake up and leave my bed. I can choose to have a great attitude or a poor attitude. I can look at life with excitement or exhaustion. I must have a positive attitude if I expect commitment from those I lead. If I do not have this leadership skill, those I lead will be *compliant but without commitment.*

- *Response.* I read an article by Chuck Swindoll in which he argued that life was not about what happens to us but rather how we respond to what happens. I might not be able to control certain negative challenges that come along, but my response can be pre-wired. I can pre-determine that I will remain confident and calm.

I salute all first responders—the firemen, EMS, police officers, and others that arrive at horrific scenes and see tragedy each and every day. They deal with fatal automobile accidents, gunshot wounds, and tragedies like the one we shall never forget—9/11. When they arrive they are always cool, calm, and collected. Inside their chest their heart is beating double time, their adrenaline is racing like a rocket ship being launched, but they keep total control of their external emotions. How? They have been pre-programmed to know that their personal response is critical in every situation. How the patient views the responder can often determine whether the patient goes into shock or even cardiac arrest. So it is for me as a leader—my response skills must be pre-programmed to hold everything together while I determine the best solution. I have determined over the years of teaching leadership skills that I can't control the personal production of others. Sure, I can teach others, I can encourage others, and most importantly I can develop a culture or environment to create growth, but ultimately I can't control others. What I can control is my personal production. Each and every day I can determine the level of commitment I wish to attain. I can set goals and schedules for my expectations. It has been demonstrated that personal production can be the best teacher and motivator. My work ethic and the degree of passion I put into a project are being observed by those under my stewardship. As a leader I must set the standard by individual enterprise.

Relationships. Being on a committee with Bill Marriott Jr. gave me a brief moment to visit with him and see how he has created such a great team at the Marriott hotels. His life follows his book that I recommended (*The Spirit to Serve*) in which he attributes much of his success to relationships. He works to have a great relationship with his general managers, his general managers work to have a great relationship with their key people and department heads, and the key people and department heads work to have a great relationship with the staff. In turn the staff works to give those who stay at Marriott a pleasant environment. When people feel you care about them, they have a stronger desire to follow your leadership.

During good times we often make the mistake of taking for granted our customers, clients, or distributors. We work much harder on attracting new people than supporting those who have proven their loyalty. Consequently, when times begin to get challenging we find how important each person becomes, and sadly we see our competitors building a stronger relationship with those clients, customers, or distributors as they move away from our base of activity.

It has become quite obvious over the years that the management-employee relationship within most corporations is lacking. We hear management question why their employees are not loyal while at the same time they are failing to create a relationship with them.

The relationship between a leader and those he is leading is crucial for securing a long-term business. How you invest your words, time, money, and energy in your employees often determines the difference between success and failure. What most seek is just to feel they are being heard. They want to know that their words do mean something and you acknowledge them. They want you to see their contribution as more important than the customer or stockholder. When you *value their effort* you *increase their loyalty*.

A great example I mentioned earlier is Southwest Airlines. When you visit with any of their flight attendants or pilots they don't hesitate to say that the management respects them. The philosophy from the top simply says the greatest asset we have is our employees. They have created the ultimate *voluntary union,* people coming to work each day enjoying what they do. The method of command and control no longer works for today's leader. Those companies that create the leadership team that excels in performance skills and in relationships will always outperform their competitors. Instead of concentrating on changing your business or marketing plan, why not focus on improving your relationship with those who execute that marketing plan? A leadership secret is found in the scriptures: be *quick to listen, slow to speak, and slow to get angry.*

Vision. It is said that all great communicators rehearse a speech mentally many times before they deliver it. Athletes like Michael Jordan or Phil Mickelson visualize their movements before they ever hit the basketball court or golf course. The Bible says, "Where there is no vision, the people perish." Leaders understand their *life must follow its vision.*

Do you remember the day you received your first paddle ball? The paddle had a long rubber band with a rubber ball attached at the end. The idea was to hit the ball against the paddle as many times as possible. Think of the paddle as your vision and the ball as your life. Wherever the paddle goes the ball has no choice but to follow.

The greatest key in programming our vision is through our words. What we speak is vital to how we form our vision. "Life and death is in the power of the tongue," says the book of Proverbs. More than once I have asked a businessperson how they are doing only to hear, "I am struggling but hopefully I can survive." Struggling, hopefully, survive? Is it shocking a year later to find this individual is faring far worse than better? There is something about the human mind; it is like a large computer with our words being the keyboard. We set the mind up for victory or defeat, success or failure. I am not talking about hype or some exaggerated expectation that follows no mature sequence, but a vision created with our words that ultimately brings about the action that will produce the desired goal. A vision without a planned action is only a fantasy.

How powerful are the words we speak? I am not a pastor, but I am a person who loves to read history in the Bible. I recently came across the ultimate challenge for a leader. It was in the book of Numbers, where a leader named Moses was trying his best to move a large group of complainers from location A to location B. Time after time the group confronted him negatively. They constantly complained about not getting what they deserved and being taken from the comforts of their homes and moved around like sheep. Moses becomes extremely frustrated and asks, "Lord, why did you give me these people? (Sounds familiar.) I am not their mother; I did not bring them into this world. They are constant complainers; they never let up. God, if this is my fate, just do me a favor: *Kill me!*"

Now that is total frustration from a leader. God tells Moses to go on back and He will take care of the challenge. A few chapters later we read that once again the people were murmuring and began saying, "Such a miserable place, we are going to die, yes we will surely die." The next words that came from God were, "Those words you have spoken to Me today shall come to pass. Your bodies shall remain in the wilderness."

Wow! Those *words you have spoken.* As leaders we must be very careful how we program our vision and the vision of those we lead. Your life has no choice but to follow your vision. Be certain yours is well-defined and positive.

Humor. Leaders must be able to laugh at themselves and never take themselves too seriously. My poor wife has spent her entire life telling people, "He's just kidding." As a leader, lighten up! There is no challenge in life worth a heart attack or stress. I have seen many business people become so stressed out they destroy relationships with their mate and children. They can't shake off the challenges and enjoy relaxing with their kids. They are home each evening present in body but lost in mind. They look like they have been given a serious drug.

On October 6, 1973, Egypt attacked the State of Israel to regain land lost in the Six Day War. The United States came to the assistance of Israel and later paid the ultimate price as the Arab nations restricted the release of oil, and what they did sell was at a very high premium. Gas stations had lines of cars several miles long as gas was rationed. The stock market crashed, unemployment went up, and the interest rate hit an all time high of 21%. America saw a decade of stagflation.

I had just begun my second year in business, marketing computers and word-processing equipment. Fighting 21% interest rates while maneuvering through the minefield of sales and marketing proved disastrous. The ultimate knife to the heart came when my equipment supplier in Italy went on a sixty-day strike. Within a few short weeks I was finished. My banker was calling me; vendors were calling me (both business and personal). My bank called my note, which of course I did not have the funds to repay, so they reminded me they also held the note on our home. We sold the house in a fire sale, and the bank put the equity money against my corporate note. So there I sat, a young entrepreneur losing it all.

I did my best to remain as calm as possible and not to upset the family, but I had no choice but to come forward and tell my wife. We had, like most young couples, financed our household effects, so I felt the best way to share the challenge was by telling my wife as we went to bed, "Honey, sleep well tonight because tomorrow Sears is coming for the bed." There was this silence; then she said, "You are just kidding, right?"

As the days progressed, our cars were repossessed and my company liquidated. I chose not to claim bankruptcy but instead to sell off all my assets and take the balance of the note personally. We moved into our new condo and had some friends over, and naturally the first words out of their mouths were, "Wow, what happened to your home?" My response was "We had an offer we just could not refuse." I determined at that young age that I would never allow anyone to kill my

BOB GOSHEN

spirit, and the best way to keep my spirit was with a sense of humor.

A leader must find humor when struggles come. Yes, at the time it may be hard to laugh, but your physical body demands a release, and if you do not obey, then sickness comes which does no one any good.

As leaders, remember these five principles that always prevail—*Basics, Control, Relationships, Vision, and Humor.* If we can remain loyal to these principles we find ourselves well-positioned for success.

Thank You for Flying with Aeroflot Airlines

I am approaching four million air miles. Most airline pilots do not have that many miles in the sky, and I have heard plenty of landing announcements, but this really caught my attention when I flew into Moscow: "Ladies and gentlemen, we know you have a choice in airlines, and we thank you for choosing Aeroflot."

As a leader, you have been given the opportunity and responsibility to lead others. Our ultimate success is determined by how well we groom and mentor potential leaders. Those who follow our leadership will ask, "Why should I want to fly with you? *Why should I follow your leadership?* What has given you the ability and qualifications to lead others?"

Sadly, university graduates who have studied business and management soon find out the degree has no value when they are given the responsibility to lead others. I have yet to find a university that goes into depth teaching people skills. They teach "management skills," but you can have the mechanics of knowledge and yet never be a leader.

Today, generations X and Y are looking for leadership, men and women who have learned and proven how to lead and become mentors; they are looking for someone they can rely on who will shoot straight. Unlike in years past, they will not respond to the standard command and control leadership, and unlike those in the past, this generation has no problem saying "see ya' around" and moving on to another company if they feel they are being misled or given improper instruction. So if I were sitting in a nice restaurant with you and asked, "Why should I be led by you?" what would be your response?

Sadly what we find in most corporations are CEOs or upper management that move people into positions of leadership based on length of employment, loyalty, or simply because the person is likeable. We witness boards and leadership teams being created by people who only agree with the leader or CEO and are not able to offer their personal insight. When you think about this it becomes obvious why so many companies seldom move forward.

I have a saying when I enter a boardroom or leadership meeting: "If everyone in this room thinks alike, someone is not needed." You get growth by surrounding yourself with the people who are strong in the areas you are weak. The challenge for a leader is to continually search for people who can add intellectual value to their company or project. Those in leadership who put their egos aside and find people stronger than

themselves become great leaders. It is your responsibility to bring life to the project or corporate culture,
and people generate life; business plans and financial
statements do not.

Taking Life from Leaders
Keeping the Spirit in your Leaders

When you strip the spirit from the horse, you lose every race. How often have we found a great group of men and women who have the fire and passion to create exceptional results? They have the commitment and ability to move the corporation to the next level only to have that fire quenched by their CEO or president. With only a few words of doubt and negative forecasting from their founder, the life begins to leave those who have proven their ability to "make things happen."

Raising purebred Egyptian Arabian horses has allowed me to become familiar with the spirit of the breed. The Arabian is very aloof, with head held high and tail arched over the back, they seem to float around the pasture. They, like great leaders, have a self-confidence that is undeniable. It is a shame to find such a beautiful animal, full of spirit, under the instruction and training of someone who does not recognize and know how to work with the positive traits of the horse. There are trainers who believe if you break the horse down, make the horse submit to a set of rules and regulations created from negative and defensive planning, the horse will submit and perform. By this method of training you get a stable horse rather than a producer.

The parallel is amazing as you observe the founders of corporations operating out of envy, jealously, and pride—demoralizing their key leaders through rules and regulations written from a position of total ignorance. Let me be more specific by sharing personal observations from my early years of working for a company.

When I came aboard as a new young salesman, I was given a minimum draw and commission. I was just making a living when I discovered a piece of equipment in the showroom that was the early concept of a desktop computer. The unit weighed about fifty pounds, and the media used to make it work was a magnetic strip card. You would program the card with mathematical symbols to have it create the proper answer in a very short period of time. I discovered that I could program this unit and have it figure installment loans for banks, along with other complicated financial equations. In a rather short period of time I hit what is called a "vertical market" and began selling two or three of these units per week. The unit with the programs sold for $5000, which back in that particular time period was a tremendous amount of money. It took me around three years to create a library of magnetic cards that handled ninety percent of all banking challenges, and when I did, I began making loads of money both for the company and me.

As my income increased, mostly driven by commissions, the owner became very jealous, as I was actually taking home more money and spending less time working than he. In his mind I was making money "too easily," and therefore, the compensation plan had to be changed in order to "bring me back in line." Now think about this, before I began moving this unit, the company was surviving at best, and due to my efforts it was now experiencing record retail sales. I was alive, excited, passionate, even began recruiting new people to assist me in the sales and programming areas.

The owner called me in on a Friday and said he was reducing my commissions and asked that I expand my hours. Amazing! He had a stallion and was working to beat him into a "stable horse," just one of the normal sales boys who barely made their quota. It happened so fast. One week I was on cloud nine, the following under a cloud of gloom.

The rule is very simple: "When you punish the producer, production will stop." He took the life from a key leader and producer. When this happens, the producer begins looking for other avenues in which to produce, and like me they often go out and create a company that becomes a competitor. Do not get caught in this trap. Whenever an owner or key leader begins to believe they need to redistribute the commissions from proven leaders to potential leaders, failure will soon follow.

Keeping Your Producers Producing

One way to keep your producers in production mode is to keep their personal dream alive. A producing leader is driven by three fundamentals: they must have a dream, believe they can achieve the dream, and believe the organization where they are employed has the product and service to make their dream reality. A producer, again, is like a spirited Arabian horse; the horse will do anything for you and will remain quite loyal as long as you remain consistent in your training and rewards. It has been proven many times that people seek recognition as much as money. It is amazing how many organizations overlook this point.

Some organizations conduct week-long conferences where entire programs seem built around extolling the virtues of the company founders or the people who planned the event. What more ideal platform could there be for recognizing the company's producers? What could be wiser than showcasing those who have proven their ability to produce, those who have gone beyond the norm when others have remained flat? People must be recognized in front of their peers when they achieve beyond the norm.

Who Motivates the Motivator?

Challenge is constant for the leader of a major corporation, a pastor, or any manager. It is often said that it is "lonely at the top," and for those in leadership positions, that's an accepted fact. The leader's primary purpose is to keep the energy flowing and dreams growing while at the same time showing up every day with a smiling face and an endless supply of new ideas and solutions for the day-to-day challenges. Often the leader may feel as if a giant syringe has been injected into his or her brain and all the energy extracted. This is reality in the world of leadership. Those who have been given the opportunity to lead must restore their minds and physical health often, for just like a car battery, one can only go so far on limited cells.

So how does the leader stay motivated and on top of the game? The following suggestions have helped many in leadership to stay focused and on fire as they move their organizations forward:

1. *Find a Mentor.* The only way to stay focused and keep energy flowing is to find a "creative mentor" who has the ability to keep the apprentice's feet grounded in leadership principles. The mentor is that person who deserves respect, who will listen to challenges, fears, hopes, and dreams, and can be trusted to keep confidences, someone who is totally honest in supporting not only the student's business or organization but also that person's total well-being, and someone who can "rationally" not

"emotionally" respond to another's busy world. A qualified mentor should fit the following parameters: he or she needs nothing from the learner, is not looking for financial benefits or special favors, must be a person of integrity and character, and, most importantly, must be a proven leader who has been where the follower is going. As I mentioned before, in Vietnam the statement was often used, "If you are going through a minefield, follow someone."

2. *Feed the Mind.* A leader is always feeding the mind. Good teachers can be found in every field of endeavor, and many of the best have produced CDs or books in their areas of expertise. They often have websites that detail or reveal their thinking processes. It isn't necessary to "reinvent the wheel" and waste months and years on subjects that have already been explored and developed. Material from the experience of the experts can be absorbed and wrapped in the thoughts and personality of the diligent student and made to work. A wise pupil will develop unique and personal ways to incorporate the materials developed by those who have a proven track record. It is often better to be an imitator than an originator, especially until one gain the personal experience required in a given field of expertise. An aspiring leader must remain progressive and proactive, always maintaining a "creative state of mind."

3. *Dreams or Drama.* I have found that most of the conversation in the working world is focused around the world of "drama." People talk about other people; people put people down while lifting themselves up. People continually look for and often hope for another person's failure. To stay motivated, one must become very sensitive to the conversation in the boardroom, at lunch with others, and even in one's own family. The leader cannot allow his or her mind to drift into the world of drama, choosing instead to remain in the arena of dreams, looking for solutions, and becoming a doctor of solutions. Those who stay personally motivated "run" from the world of conversation that moves toward destructive thoughts and behavior. They choose words that are edifying, building up those around them each day, addressing "challenges" rather than "problems." It is difficult to stay motivated and on top of one's game if hours are wasted in the world of drama, especially since most of the leader's time is spent in the area of counseling and helping others to become better. Like a good bomb technician, the leader learns how to quickly disengage from conversation that is drama.

4. *Enjoy.* Motivated people take time to enjoy the world around them. They spend time with people who do not wish to talk about their profession or business; they know how to have

fun and enjoy fellowship with people who make them laugh. They talk about the things in their lives that are humorous; they listen to those outside of their field of endeavor who are willing to share what they have learned of life skills. A truly successful leader knows that time spent with family and loved ones is as essential as time spent with those who add value to their profession. Those closest to the leader will not be impressed with his or her balance sheet. They will not care if the leader has added value to the business or organization if it is accomplished at the expense of their needs and desires. They *will* be impressed if the leader expends as much energy entering their personal world as he or she does digging into a marketing plan or business plan or next week's message. A leader who desires to stay motivated will learn to be spontaneous in personal affairs, sharing the world of their children's dreams if they are parents, planning memorable outings with their spouse if they are married, being active listeners with their friends and companions.

The life of a leader can be very hectic and demanding. By virtue of their professions, leaders live in the crosshairs of human needs. But if they fail to take care of their personal well-being and the well-being of those close to them, they will have failed at their most important leadership position, that of being a husband, father, wife, mother, and friend.

Stealing Life and Joy from Leaders

As a leader you must be quick to define the four areas that can take life from your leadership and take away the joy of leading others.

Pride. It has been said that "pride precedes the fall of man," and I find that to be true. If you read your own press and others constantly tell you how great you are, you can develop pride that will ultimately destroy your leadership. It is important to be proud of your accomplishments, but not at the expense of others. I have yet to find a man or a woman who has accomplished anything without direct or indirect help from others. Accept your leadership status from a position of favor and grace rather than personal ability. Stay humble, never take yourself too seriously, and always recognize those around you who have elevated you to your current position.

Plans. A leader's value increases in direct proportion to the unscheduled changes and interruptions he encounters. Your value as a leader is not only in your area of expertise but more importantly in how you respond to the daily changes and challenges. I have seen leaders begin their day on track, happy, full of joy and delight; then a curveball is thrown at them and they begin a meltdown process. Consistency and joy must remain in good times and bad times.

People. Leaders cannot allow the destructive criticism from others to derail their direction and focus. Not all of your decisions will be accepted by your subordinates, and often you will find yourself criticized for a decision you have made. Leaders can lose their joy and drive when this occurs if they do not have a strong belief in their decision-making capabilities. As a leader your job is not to work to please others; it is to make decisions that will move the cause forward without hurting others. Determine today that your leadership will be based on *principles*, not on what people think.

Problems. A common belief is that life should be problem free. I often ask when speaking, "How many in the audience had a problem last week? How many in the audience have a problem this week? How many believe they are going to have a problem next week?" The hands always go up. As a leader you do not look forward to problems, but like a good emergency medical technician you are ready for them. During rainstorms in Houston it always amazes me to see five or six wreckers lined up under an overpass. They are like vultures circling dying animals, waiting for their prey, in this case the next pile up. As leaders we should not get up every morning looking for problems, but at the same time we should not be alarmed when they arrive. And we can never let the problem take away the joy of leading. You are in a position of leadership for a reason: your ability to respond to problems.

Riveted Focus
97% vs. 3% rule

Have you ever asked, "Why is it that some people become great leaders and others never make it?" What truly separates the achiever from the non-achiever? Is it education? Good looks? DNA?

Why is it that there always seem to be those few who achieve a higher level of accomplishment or success? Is it because they are more intelligent? Were they simply at the right place at the right time? Could it be their personality? Did they attend the correct college? Were their parents great leaders? Could it be their physical appearance or the social environment that paved their way? The answers to these questions might give us some insight into their past, but they will not reveal why they became great leaders.

A dear friend of mine, Dr. Bruce Ewing, an outstanding leader and frequent chapel speaker for professional athletes, shares a story that offers tremendous insight into the "why."

"I will never forget that cold Sunday morning in Cleveland, Ohio, before the war between the Cleveland Browns and the world champion Green Bay Packers. One could not help but be overwhelmed by the concentration and focus of each player as he walked in for the 9:30 chapel service. You could feel the intensity as players entered carrying their playbook, some their Bible, for the twenty-minute spiritual encouragement. Perhaps there has never been such a gathering of future hall of fame inductees as that—Bart Starr, Willie Wood, Willy Davis, Carroll Dale, Travis Williams and Ray Nitschke, just to mention a few.

What was it that set these men apart from the rest? Certainly there were others who had more talent, more magnetic personalities, and certainly were better looking. What was it about these athletes that produced more than a successful game or successful year, but a successful career? After chapel, I had the opportunity to ask many of them that question. And the answer? *Focus!* They had been coached and trained to bring every thought captive to their purpose, not just on game day. Not just at practice. It was a 24/7 focus that dictated every decision and thought of those who 'made it.' These men lived in a world filled with continual distractions, yet those who made it had one thing in common: *a riveted focus on their purpose.*"

As leaders we are challenged every hour of the day, the more growth the more challenges. The distractions come from all directions: family, friends, financial, health, and from those we lead. I have found two things helpful in handling distractions.

1. *Identify your diversions.* The earlier in the day you can identify anticipated diversions and put them at the top of your "to do" list, the better. Identify items that have the potential to steal your focus and productivity.

2. *Filter your thinking.* Filter each potential diversion through a pre-determined thought process: "When I am dealing with this diversion I must remain positive not negative; I must remain focused, and I will work to edify those who come in contact with me." A leader should never be surprised when diversions come throughout the day. Stay riveted on your focus, and you will remain in the creative mindset needed to move forward.

Observation

Over my years I have followed the people who excel as great leaders. I have developed what I call the ultimate 3% rule, the characteristics that distinguish the top 3% of leadership. They break down as follows:

3%	97%
Expect Challenges	Overwhelmed when Challenged
Internally Driven	Externally Controlled
Visionary	Blinded by Daily Obstacles
Expect to Win	Hope to Win
Recover Quickly and Move On	Hold on to Past Failures
Edify Others with Words and Action	Destroy with Words and Actions
Control Environment	Controlled by Environment
Riveted Focus on Purpose	Continually Trying to Locate Focus

The 3% characteristics are dominant in the great leaders I have known. I don't think any of those leaders get up each morning and look forward to challenges, but they are never surprised when a challenge occurs. Seldom would they say, "I can't believe this is happening to me." Instead they say, "It's happening; let's find the solution and get on with life."

As I shared earlier in the book, but feel it is important enough to say again, the top 3% are totally internally driven. They don't ignore outside circumstances and they acknowledge unanticipated changes in their business environment, but they do not let the *external* drive them *internally*. Like a good pilot in turbulence, they tighten their seat belt and hold true to their direction.

They are tremendous visionaries. They are the ones who often wake up in the middle of the night with a new idea or marketing concept. They get up, grab a piece of paper, and do a quick outline in order to review the thought the next morning. They seem to be very flexible as they move their vision toward completion, understanding there will be additional items that must be added or deleted in order to make the vision come true. They can picture the completion of their vision sometimes years before it comes to pass.

Walt Disney was a great visionary, but the greatest tribute to Mr. Disney came at the opening of Disney World. After the completion of Disneyland, Mr. Disney had the vision of something even more grand and spectacular. Sadly, Mr. Disney passed away prior to the completion of Disney World. The story goes that on the day for the ribbon cutting at Disney World, the top executives were on the platform when one of the men turned to his associate and said, "I sure wish Walt was here to see this," to which the colleague responded, "Walt did see it or it would not be here." Oh the power of the vision!

The top 3% *expect* to win instead of *hoping* to win. I think the best way to demonstrate this point is to ask you to focus on something you would like to see come to completion and repeat our *hope versus expect* exercise. Let's say your goal is to have a 10% increase in profits for the coming year. Say out loud to yourself,

"I hope to have a 10% profit this coming year." Now say, "I *expect* to have a 10% profit for the coming year." I am confident you found more energy in the second statement. The mind begins to take away all room for failure, while in the first statement the mind can always set up a way for escape to justify the failure. As a once famous statement at NASA goes: "Failure is not an option."

I am often asked to explain mentoring. Replace the word "mentoring" with "equipping" and the meaning becomes quite clear. We are to equip those who are under the influence of our leadership and ensure they not only have the performance skills necessary to accomplish their goals and dreams but that they have developed the 3% characteristics.

It's So Easy but Yet So Hard

In 1991 I was retained by a major corporation to circle the world training their distributors, customer service representatives, and general managers. I had just finished the development and implementation of "Partners in Education" for Coca-Cola. While working with Coca-Cola I had the unique pleasure of meeting many great men and women in the marketing department and often would hear them give great reviews to the former CEO, Robert W. Woodruff. He was described by many as a tremendous leader and was very personable with everyone at Coca-Cola.

I remember one day the department head gave me a little booklet written by Mr. Woodruff. It was given to everyone who worked at Coca-Cola. It contained brilliant insights, including this one that still sticks with me:

> "Life is pretty much a selling job. Whether we succeed or fail is largely a matter of how well we motivate the human beings with whom we deal to buy us and what we have to offer. Success or failure in this job is essentially a matter of human relationships. It is a matter of the kind of reaction to us by our family, members, customers, employees, and fellow workers and associates. If this reaction is favorable we are quite likely to succeed. If the reaction is unfavorable we are doomed. The deadly sin in our relationship with people is that we take them for granted. We do not make an active or continuous effort to do and say things that will make them like us, and believe us, and that will create in them the desire to work with us in the attainment of our desires and purposes. Again and again, we see both individuals and organizations perform only to a small degree of their potential success, or fail entirely, simply because of their neglect of the human element in business and life. They take people and their actions for granted. Yet, it is these people and their responses that make or break us."

Another consistent thread you will find running through every successful leader is the ability to develop relationships. They focus on the needs of others and they continually reinforce and encourage everyone they meet. Leaders understand that success and failure are dependent on the relationships developed both within their organization and outside it. Those who fail in leadership development will also score poorly in relationship development. As a leader you must work daily to maintain a close relationship with those in your organization who have proven their leadership ability.

As Stanley C. Allyn put it, "The most useful person in the world today is the man or woman who knows how to get along with other people. Human relations is the most important science in living."

Your View of Leadership

As a leader your most significant accomplishment will be mentoring those who become leaders. Let us look at a couple of factors that can slow the process of becoming a leader.

How you view those you are leading. A traveler nearing a great city asked an old man seated by the road, "What are the people like in this city?" The old man replied, "What were they like where you came from?" "Horrible," the traveler reported. "Mean, untrustworthy, detestable in all respects." "Ah," said the old man, "you will find them the same in the city ahead."

Scarcely had the first traveler gone on his way when another stopped to inquire about the people in the city before him. The old man said, "What were they like where you came from?" The traveler responded, "They were fine people, honest, industrious and generous. I was sorry to leave." The old man responded, "That's exactly how you'll find the people here."

The way people see others is a reflection of themselves. If I am a trusting person, I will see others as trustworthy. If I am a critical person, I will see others as critical. And if I am a caring person, I will see others as compassionate. As leaders developing leaders, we must look at those we are mentoring for leadership from the eyes of great expectation. Let us never forget this simple story.

They come with baggage. As a leader developing leaders, you will often need to help them drop old baggage. Some have come from a negative environment and come to us needing positive belief instilled. We all have a personal frame of reference that consists of our attitudes, assumptions, and expectations. These factors determine whether we're optimistic or pessimistic, cheerful or gloomy, trusting or suspicious, friendly or reserved, brave or timid. Dr. Phil McGraw said, "You teach people how to treat you."

It Begins with Ideas

Everything begins with an idea. Leaders understand that they are constantly in the battle of the mind—first seeking to reform their thinking, then looking for a better execution of plans. A leader says, "I *have* to have it, it's *got* to happen. I am going to *make* it happen. I am passionate, I am driven, and I am going to make this work." But the passage of time and involvement in many projects can dilute that original passion for the project. Pro-active thinking gives way to defensive thinking, or once again without even realizing it, the leader moves to survival mode. A project is in trouble when leaders hear themselves utter the words, "Oh, I'm not doing badly." As a leader you have earned the reputation of having the ability to do better. Moreover, you have the responsibility to do better. Eleanor Roosevelt said, "Great minds discuss ideas, average minds discuss events, small minds discuss people." Where is your mind today?

I had the unique opportunity to do the morning devotional for the Zig Ziglar Corporation. As you read in my acknowledgments, Zig has been my mentor for years. At the end of the meeting it was just me, Zig, and his wonderful personal assistant, Laurie Magers. We started talking about marriage, and Mr. Zig said the following, "Bob, if men would court their wives after marriage as much as they did before marriage, there would never be need for a divorce.

Oh How Fresh

How sweet and precious is a newborn baby!

How sweet is the smell inside a new car!

How fresh was our love when we first got married!

Then it happens—we have two or three babies and they begin to grow up and bounce from corner to corner in the house, they jump on the sofa and lose the TV remote, and we forget about how fresh was the sight of that newborn face. When the car was new we parked it three blocks away from the main door of the movie theatre. It was washed once or twice a week, but after a short time it loses that new car freshness, and we would rather consider a door ding than a long walk. Oh yes, the marriage. Those first weeks, months, and even a year are nothing but bliss and happiness. We set up the house, we arrange the furniture, define the placement of articles in the bathroom with all sorts of love and kindness. Then the freshness of the new marriage mellows; the consideration of opening a door or holding hands wherever you go is gone. The bathroom becomes a battleground as we discuss how long to keep the tube of toothpaste. We allow the freshness of the new to somehow slip away.

Just as we can often lose the freshness of a newborn baby, new car, or marriage, we can begin to lose the freshness of what was considered the ideal marketing plan or business concept. I am confident that many of the great ideas have been filed away in organizations around the globe because they "lost their freshness."

As leaders, our responsibility is to keep freshness in the ideas, in the projects, and most importantly in the people who are called to carry out the plans. We must wake up each day and breathe freshness into the marketing plan or the business model that we know can go to the top. When we as leaders lose the ability to breathe freshness into dreams and plans, our value is no longer needed. Oh how sweet it is to keep the freshness in our ideas.

Do We Have the Correct Players?

What are you doing today to be proactive? I have found that many projects fail because the leader didn't recognize that some team members were not measuring up. Instead of pulling them out of the process, the leader continued to work with them and even cover for them. Leaders must realize that they are responsible *to* people but not *for* people. We must have the players on the team who have the *will to win*.

A leader understands that often the only thing standing between a successful project and a failed project is the *will to try it* and the *faith to believe it.* Belief is not an idea one possesses. It's an idea that possesses us. "I can move forward with this idea! I can create the execution strategy to make this concept work!" As a leader you must get possessed by that. The first and most important step toward success has always been the *expectation that you can succeed.*

Ben Franklin, a wise old man, once said, "Blessed is he who expects nothing, for he will receive it." There is no way we can move forward if negative expectations are part of our thinking process. Negative expectations are the quickest route to destruction, to the death of a project.

William James said, "That which holds our attention determines our action." Wow! Think about this statement, and I suggest repeating it out loud several times. The freshness of a project, the expectation to succeed, demands our attention. Perhaps some of you in leadership need to examine your thinking. I want you to open up the lid on your brain. Leaders have no room for the survival mentality. Return to the day when you first had this incredible idea for a project. Think of the excitement when you first put the idea on paper and began adding all the fundamentals that would breathe life into it. Go back and reflect on the passion you had at the beginning. Remember your thinking process before you put walls around the idea. Donald Trump said, "You have to think anyway, you might as well think *big.*" As leaders we must always remain fresh, think big, and tear down the walls.

Why There Are Only 22 Seats in First Class
Mediocrity Cannot Sit Up Front

I was raised in very modest conditions. Our first home was around 400 square feet. It had a combination living room and kitchen, and my sisters and I shared a bedroom with our parents. The door to our bathroom was a cloth curtain, and the toilet sat on one side of the wall with the sink directly in front of it. It was very convenient; you could brush your teeth while going to the bathroom.

Not only did we have bunk beds but bunk chairs sitting on top of one another. As one person said, we had to go outside just to change our mind. As I became a little older, we moved up to a 600-square-foot home, and by my senior year in high school we had hit the 900-square-foot capacity. I will never forget when I was thirteen going with my father each Friday night to take the mail to the downtown post office. There were times I would look out of the window and see these incredible homes with luxury cars parked in front of them. I would ask my father how those folks created that sort of living. He would often respond by saying, "Oh, don't get too excited about those folks, just think how much their electric bill might be;" or "Can you imagine how long it would take to clean that house?" Such fine motorcars would pass us, and I can never forget seeing my first Rolls Royce and telling my father, "Wow!" "Think of the gasoline that car uses," he replied.

Looking back I now understand his was sort of a defensive response given so I would not get my hopes up about having the better things in life. He did not want us to get disappointed in the future. But I will never forget the one question that triggered my initial investigation into those of financial influence. I once saw a beautiful mansion in Tulsa. It was magnificent; the grounds were lush, and the home so large and stately and once again I gave that big "Wow, Dad, look at that!" The response was, "Yes, the rich just get richer."

In my little mind I asked the simple question, "If that is true, why not study the wealthy to see what their habits might be?" Now let's stay on track. I am not suggesting that success is defined by how much money one has. I know many people of substantial wealth who lead very stressful and unfulfilling lives. My thinking was not about how to achieve wealth but about learning the habits that are productive in order to excel in life. At that point I began doing research, reading biography after biography of men and women of influence, and I have not stopped doing so to this day.

Several years ago I was retained by a large distribution company in California to assist in the development of their leadership team. The company grew rapidly from around $250 million to $800 million in sales, and we were contacted by *The Wall Street Journal* about doing a story.

I met with the journalist in a boardroom, just him and me, and he began asking many questions about the company and the business. One question went something like this, "What does the average new business owner do in the company?" My response was, "Average business people quit. Average business people will not stay the course, because most average business people live the life of mediocrity."

Have you ever noticed how many seats are in the first class compartment of an airplane? Depending on whether it is domestic or international the number will vary, but normally on an international flight you will find around twenty-two seats. Have you ever wondered who came up with this number and why? Someone way before our time determined that only a few people would step out and succeed. Look at the tax system in the United States and you will discover that a small percentage of people pay the majority of taxes. Average people and people living the life of mediocrity will not move into leadership, and if by some rare case they do become leaders, the journey will be short. The characteristics required to be a leader do not include mediocrity; the person in leadership has no "quit" in him or her. My life-long research on why some succeed at leadership and others do not has proven that "average" is not in the DNA of a leader.

Taking a Survey

Since I fly a great deal internationally, I decided to do a quick survey of those in first class to get an idea of what they do and if possible a brief history. How did they get one of the twenty-two seats? What were some of the common characteristics?

Very few were born into wealthy families. The majority came from modest backgrounds, from both single-parent families and strong family units. They were not the sharpest in their high school or college classes; most were "C" average students. They did not see themselves as doing anything great, but mostly being in the right position at the right time, recognizing it, and taking advantage of it.

I thought the words "recognizing it" were most enlightening. We often find people who have been put in the right position at the right time but never recognize it. They have an opportunity that can greatly impact their future, but they walk right by it. In leadership I find this to be one of the separations between a good leader and a great leader. The great leader recognizes how to respond to a situation, where the good leader just does not have the ability to see everything.

Second, none were narcissistic. For the most part they played down their achievements. They had a healthy respect for themselves and a strong confidence in what they were capable of doing, but they did not see themselves as being super special or some sort of a star.

It was apparent that those interviewed in the first class compartment were highly focused on what they were doing. I remember visiting with a young man who worked for a very reputable accounting firm. He was in his late thirties and had already moved into a very high-profile leadership position. He had thirteen accountants under his leadership. When I asked him about his dedication to the job, and especially after seeing him work on his computer the first three hours of the flight, he made it clear that he was willing to go out and do what he was asking his fellow accountants to do. His personal example was the best leadership tool in his arsenal.

Across the board, the common theme among all interviewed was "I am not going to ask those I lead to do a task that I am not personally willing to do." Leadership demands mentorship, always performing the task that you ask others to perform. Ivory tower leadership is a fallacy, and those who practice such activity will soon find themselves falling from the tower.

And lastly, each and every person loved what he or she did. They woke up each morning looking forward to the new challenges. They loved the interaction with those they were leading. Their greatest challenge, in their own words, was keeping it all in balance. They loved their careers so much they had to force themselves to "leave it at the office." It was amazing to find that the majority had the ability to transfer their "work ethics" to "play ethics," focusing just as much energy on having fun with family and friends as on pursuing their careers.

Knowing the Truth

In the movie *A Few Good Men,* Mr. Jack Nicholson delivers the famous line, "You want the truth? You can't handle the truth." Well, as leaders we must never forget that the truth and only the truth keeps us free.

I have spent years studying those who have become successful in all areas of life, and I have found that many of the things we are taught in school (and even by our parents and friends) about achievers are simply not true. Over the past two decades, we seem to have created a mindset in our high schools and colleges that success and true free enterprise are more of a liability than an asset.

In Australia they have a phrase called the "poppy syndrome," which literally means to really stand up or stand out. On the other hand, when I conduct leadership seminars in Sweden, I have to focus on getting the participants to believe it is okay to stand up and take control of one's life. In Sweden they really do not talk about achieving wealth or success, so I have reformatted my seminars to share how life can be better if one has more money to give to those who have less. In both cases, my listeners had to feel good about themselves or they would never develop the leadership skills required to advance their cause or execute their business plan.

We must make sure that "achievement" is never taken out of the vocabulary of the American school system. Young people must understand that they have the ability to become great leaders and they can achieve their personal dreams through the free enterprise system that has created more success than any system on the planet.

While in Moscow, Russia, I read in the morning paper that Vladimir Putin spoke to the banking industry and made the comment that the Russian government needs to let go of the controls on private business and move more companies into the free market, because only the free market can restore Russia to a stronger existence.

Those are sobering words coming from a former KGB leader and words that we must never forget in the United States. America is where it is today because of the leaders it has produced. We must remember that without the free market and leaders who are committed to capitalism, America has the capacity to fall.

The current news all over Europe is how socialism is failing and conservative parties are taking back control. This is a major lesson for leaders: we must keep close to our hearts the importance of *enterprise over entitlement* and *self-reliance over government reliance*. As leaders we must filter our decisions through this sifter: Are we teaching our future leaders how to be self-governed and accountable for their actions? Are we teaching them that enterprising thinking creates people who believe in themselves, and that the only entitlement we have is to make ourselves better human beings?

Goal Setting

My wife says, "A dream without action only equals a fantasy." A dream has very little value. One must attach feet to the dream—the goals.

Goals are actually "driven by the dream" and must be very precise and clear. A businessperson who has just established a new business and marketing plan might say, "I wish to employ 100 people by the end of the year. I wish to hit one million dollars in profit by my second year in business." A pastor might say, "I wish to have a particular piece of land purchased by the end of the year, or I expect my congregation to have 1,000 members within the next eight months." The profession does not matter; it only matters that goals are set and a date assigned to them.

I had read that fewer than 7% of people ever write out their goals and even fewer have a dream. If this is correct, why should we be shocked to see so many fail in leadership, living in a survival mode instead of success? What I share is so simple yet seemingly so profound to many. There are so many books written on goal setting that I really did not want to linger on the topic in this book. However, almost everyone I interviewed on the various flights shared the importance of goal setting. So let me briefly share my insight on this topic as it relates to leadership.

Some of us may have set so many goals that never came to pass that we no longer even attempt to, or even worse we create goals with no expectation of achieving them. Let me share three brief points that hopefully you will consider:

1. Write down the goal.

2. Write down *why* you need that goal.

3. Write the down the *plan* for achieving that goal.

As elementary as this may sound, many people never write down their goals. And those who do often *just* write down the goal. They never write down the *why*. And without the why the goal will never be achieved.

Someone might say, "I want to lose thirty pounds." Why? "Because I want to look good." Why? "Well, because I can." Why? Keep asking "Why do I have to achieve this goal?" We must keep asking ourselves why to find the *main* reason for achieving the goal.

Often our goal setting is determined by external thoughts or people, but for a goal to be achieved it must be *internal*. We must give birth to the *why*. In an earlier chapter I said, "When you take the creator out of the creation, the creation will die." We must create our personal goals; we must birth them. We are the only ones who have the capacity to bring our goals to completion. Write them down and place dates on their projected completion.

Your Choice

Each day we make choices. We choose what time we get out of bed, what clothes we are going to wear, what time we are going to leave the house, in what order we are going to respond to our to-do list. Each day literally hundreds of choices must be made, and a leader could surely double that number.

You are reading this book in hopes of becoming a leader, or you have purchased the book to sharpen your leadership skills—another choice. As leaders we must realize we will never get it all done, and we will never be completely satisfied with our efforts, for we have been given that internal commitment of "doing better" and getting the job done more efficiently.

You have chosen to step up and become a leader, or perhaps you have stumbled into a position of influence because those above you moved on. No matter how you have achieved the position, you are there. You must now choose how you wish to lead, how to create the environment to create leaders within your team. It's time to step up to one of the twenty-two seats. It's time to locate those who desire to be leaders, to equip and develop them to the best of your ability, and to layer leadership by duplicating yourself in others.

We as leaders must understand the importance of developing leaders under leaders, a layered leadership that will continue after we are gone. The best example of this is a story about the famous general, George Patton. As he was ready to enter a battle in Europe, he asked all of his company commanders to come to his tent. He stood in front of them and he asked, "Men, what constitutes a leader?" One by one each company commander stood and gave his definition of leadership, to which General Patton would respond in his straightforward no nonsense voice, "You're wrong; sit down."

After the last man expressed his definition, Patton donned his helmet, shoved his baton into his belt, and stood to address his men. "Gentlemen, a leader must be able to be shot and killed and never missed. Let's move out."

If we focus on locating leaders, providing a positive environment for developing and duplicating leaders, and if we give them the freedom to flourish, we will have produced what I call layered leadership. Let's move out!